G000168165

A 'RAC AGAINST TIME?

social services provision to black elders

NAINA PATEL

Race and Policy Series No 1

The
Runnymede
Trust

Acknowledgements

An inspiration from my parents greatly aroused my interest and concern in social service provision to black elders. The decision to undertake research into this area was further motivated by my desire to use this opportunity to provide a synthesis of various empirical studies within a sound analysis of British racism. Much of this book is based on research undertaken as part of my Master's dissertation and I would like to reiterate my thanks to all those who helped me in that task.

I am particularly grateful to Hafiz Mirza who has been my greatest support. He provided an ideal environment for intense debate, exchange of ideas, meals — and read my draft with a critical eye! My special thanks also to Charles Husband for his valuable guidance, critical comments and encouragement which helped me to complete this study.

I feel extremely privileged that an organisation whose many publications over the years have been an important source of influence in shaping my thoughts and ideas on "race" and racism should publish this work. My warm thanks to the Runnymede Trust and its Director, Ken Leech. I am very grateful to David Rosenberg, Publications Officer, whose expert sub-editing and advice have helped to produce this book.

Naina Patel
March 1990

The Runnymede Trust gratefully acknowledges the financial support of the Triangle Trust towards the costs of producing this publication.

Published by the Runnymede Trust
11 Princelet Street, London E1 6QH
June 1990
ISBN 0 902397 84 2
© Runnymede Trust 1990
Designed by David Rosenberg
Typeset and printed by the Russell Press, Nottingham
Cover photographs: Max Farrar

Contents

Preface   iv

1. Introduction   1
2. Black elders in a historical context   9
3. Who cares for the black elders?   16
4. The invisibility factor   30
5. A conceptual framework   35
6. A separate or mainstream existence?   51

Postscript   59

Bibliography   64

List of tables, graphs and diagrams

Tables

1.1 The age-sex structure of "industrialised" and "developing" regions   2
1.2 Trends in Britain for persons aged 60 years and over, 1985-2011   3
1.3 Population by ethnic group and age   7
2.1 Employment and immigration 1956-60   10
2.2 "Immigrant" workers as a percentage of the total workforce by industry   12
3.1 Key studies of black elders 1981-1987   17
3.2 Knowledge of services by "ethnic" group   19
3.3 Use of services   20
3.4 Rejection of services   20
3.5 Health problems reported by the elders, by "ethnic" group   25
4.1 Household composition by "ethnic" group from three surveys   32

Graph

3.1 Black elders' usage of services   28

Diagrams

5.1 A conceptual framework for the analysis of British racism and its consequences particularly at the organisational level   37
5.2 The position of black elders in the structure of British society   50

Preface

When elders are discussed in Britain today they are frequently lumped together as a homogeneous and insignificant group of "those who are over 60 years of age". They are simply referred to as "the elderly" and, though class divisions may be acknowledged, little concern is expressed on "race" or "gender" related issues.

It is estimated that there are some 97,000 black elders — not an insignificant number by any means. A few academics, black practitioners and organisations have attempted to bring issues concerning black elders to the fore in political and social agendas. There are many parallels with the elders in general. But, there still exist many specific areas of concern, arising mainly from the experience and consequences of racism. There is certainly much scope for study and research on service provision for black elders, consequent policy making and action for change.

1. Introduction

*"Forty is the old age of youth
fifty is the youth of old age".
(French proverb).*

The present world population is estimated at 4.5 billion. Approximately 10 per cent of the world's population is regarded as "old" (classified as 60+). The experience of ageing cuts across all class, "race" and gender divides. What differs across the globe are the values, beliefs and practices associated with those growing old. In some societies elders are assigned a high status, seen as givers of wisdom. As a Hindi saying goes: "an old person's teaching sets the world aright". In others, the elders are considered a burden, to the family, to the society — neither wanted nor needed. "In society's eyes the aged person is no more than a corpse under suspended sentence" said Simone de Beauvoir — a comment that strikes a familiar chord in Britain. If the plight of the UK's older population is considerable, that of one section — the black elders — is arguably even greater. This study seeks to analyse the position of this latter group with respect to the existing and necessary services provided by social services departments in local authorities. Before such an analysis can take place the issue must be placed in context. This chapter, therefore, examines the overall characteristics of the elders, with some emphasis on the black section of this group. Chapter 2 then discusses the historical and socio-economic background to the major issues associated with being black (and elderly) in Britain today.

The demographic facts

The UK has the largest proportion of the population aged 60 or over within the EC — but is not unique in experiencing the ageing of population. Table 1.1 shows the significant ageing of the world population expected over the next forty years.

In Europe, people over 65 accounted for 10 per cent of the population

1

Table 1.1: *The Age-Sex Structure of "Industrialised" and "Developing" Regions*

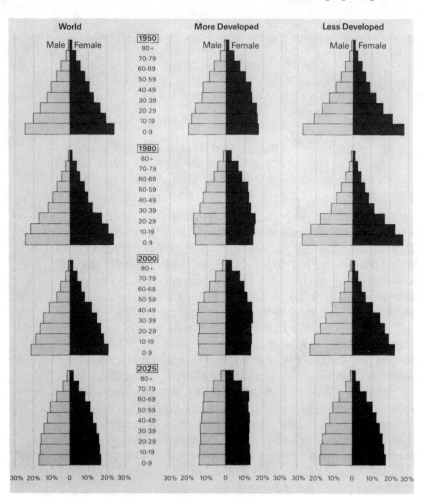

Source: *Barclays Review, February 1984.*

soon after the Second World War. Today they represent approximately 15 per cent of the total population and by the early 21st Century, one out of every five Europeans will be elderly. For Britain, the number of people aged 60 or over increased as a proportion of the population from around 6 per cent in 1901 to nearly 20 per cent in 1981. In contrast, children aged under 15 constituted 30 per cent of the population in 1901 compared to 20 per cent in 1981 (though there was an increase in the birth rate over the 1955-1965 period). These changes have to some extent off-set each other, so the percentage of the "dependent/non-active" population has been fairly stable over the long run.

The resident population of 60 or over in Britain was estimated to be at 11.4 million in 1985, of which 3 out of every 5 persons were women. Approximately 1.5 million people, mostly men aged 60-64, were economically active. Table 1.2 shows that the projections for those 60 and above reflect relative stability in the total number of persons in this age group to the end of this century. However, the balance of different age groups is expected to change in the short term: the number of people in their

Table 1.2: *Trends in Britain for persons aged 60 years and over, 1985-2011*

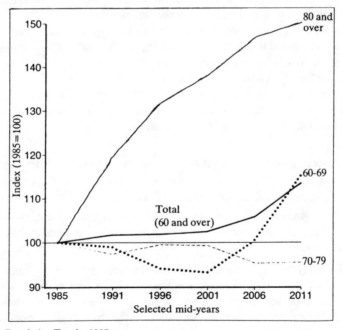

Source: *Population Trends, 1987.*

60s will decline but the number of people aged 80 years or over is estimated to rise from 1.8 million in 1985 to 2.4 million in the year 2001 and 2.6 million in 2011.

Two main factors explain these changes in the age structure:

— A consequence of the past number of births. For example, the rise in the population aged 80 or over, is a consequence of the high annual birth rate early this century.

— Increasing life expectancy: in the 1950s the expectation of life was 69 years, today it is 74 years and by 2020 it is projected to reach 77 years.

As the need for care and support increases with age, the growth in total needs of the 80 or over age-group will be critical, despite the relatively low increase of the absolute number of people. *Social Trends* (1988) aptly summarises this changing age structure and its consequence:

> "Although the size of the dependent population in 2025 will not be much higher than it was in 1971, its composition will be different in that there will be far less children and many more elderly people, so reducing demand for education but increasing the burden on health services".

Note the change in emphasis: for children, it is a "demand" for education; for the elderly, it is a "burden" on the health services!

These trends in population composition have given rise to expressions such as "the grannie boom", the "greying explosion", "the demographic winter", all symbolising negative aspects of what it means to be "old". The equation of higher expectancy of life and low birth rate, which leads to a rise in the number of older people, resulting in a greater number of dependants, which creates a greater "burden", continues to gain currency. It is often forgotten that the elders are only a financial burden to society if we assume that:

— they have made no contribution to society's growth and development;

— they have not paid for their retirement during their working lives in the form of taxes and national insurance contributions;

— technology remains constant, yielding no additional change in society's structure of work and the labour employed, income and public goods and services.

In particular, even a slowly growing economy (eg 2 per cent per annum) can finance a greatly expanded service for the elders *and* ensure constantly rising incomes for the remaining population. Consider the analogy of manufacturing versus the services sector: the former is contracting in employment terms, yet it can still "fund" the expanding "non-productive" services sector — because of rising productivity. The real issue is not absolute welfare, but rather the relative distribution of incomes. What is required then, is a complete change in the equation: an approach that radically challenges the very notion of dependence which strips the old of their dignity, independence and well-being — to demand services that are theirs as of right.

The myths and stereotyping of the ageing population have led to the concept "ageism", a term coined by Butler (1968) as:

"A process of systematic stereotyping of and discrimination against people because they are old . . . Ageism allows the younger generations to see older people as different from themselves; thus they subtly cease to identify with their elders as human beings".

In the last few years, we have witnessed a growing public awareness of the increasing number of the elders, a growth in research and books in gerentology. And yet, the experiences of the black elders have largely been neglected until quite recently, with a few publications beginning in the '70s.[1] However, despite some important books, research reports and articles produced in the last eight years on the black elderly, it cannot be described as a growth industry. Some radical writers have also contributed to the neglect by failing to consider the "race" dimension though class and gender are appropriately considered.[2]

The experience of the black elderly in Britain emphasises the double disadvantage of being poor (in income, housing, health, status and role) and a member of a minority group which suffers racial discrimination. This perspective is conceptualised as the "double jeopardy hypothesis", Dowd and Bengtson (1978) explain:

"The minority aged are said to bear, in effect, a double burden. Like other older people in industrial societies, they experience the devaluation of old age found in most modern societies . . . Unlike other older people, however, the minority aged must bear the additional economic, social and psychological burdens of living in a society in which racial equality remains more a myth than social policy.

In addition to 'race' and age, gender and social class are also important dimensions to inequality which can be incorporated in the double jeopardy hypothesis. These factors when operating together are often referred to as triple, quadruple, or multiple jeopardies describing the black elders.

---

1. The main surveys are outlined in Chapter 3, page 17. Also see the extensive references in the bibliography.
2. Amongst others, for example, see C Phillipson's highly stimulating book: *Capitalism and the Construction of Old Age*, Macmillan, 1982.

5

The black population

According to the annual Labour Force Survey, during the period 1984-6, about 2.43 million (4.5 per cent) of the total population in Britain, were from ethnic minorities. Table 1.3 indicates the distribution of the population by age and ethnicity.

By 1986 about 4 per cent of the ethnic minority population had reached retirement age (60 or over); that is around 97,280 persons. This included about 38,000 persons of Indian origin, 32,000 of either West Indian or Guyanese origins; 7,940 Pakistani, 1,030 Bangladeshi and 5,750 Chinese origins. The data does not illuminate gender differences but according to Fenton (1987), because of the differences in migration patterns "men will outnumber women among the black elderly".

The differing age structures largely reflect the pattern of migration. Most black elders of today entered the UK as young adults, while the 43 per cent UK-born blacks are regarded as the "first or second generation" children of these elders. Chapter 2 examines the nature of black migration to Britain in its historical context.

In 1986 there were an estimated 120,000 residents (aged 65 or over) living in homes provided by local authorities compared to 112,000 living in Registered Voluntary and Private Homes. "Meals on Wheels" represented two-thirds of all meals served in personal social services in 1986 (*Social Trends* 1988). Do the 97,280 black elders benefit from these and other services provided by the statutory authorities? Social Services Departments (SSDs) are by far the largest providers of services to the elders: in an institution or care at home. We will consider the needs of black elders and SSDs' response to these, in Chapter 3. In Chapters 4 and 5 we will provide an analytical model of forms of racism and their consequences in providing for the analysis of SSD responses to black elders' rights and needs for service provision.

Various reports in the last eight years have specified a clear case for change in the service delivery to the black elders. We shall look at some of these empirical studies and the demands of black elders in the context of separate care based on self-help groups or an "integrated" system within the mainstream of care which is appropriate and adequate as defined by black elders. We will, however, locate this discussion within current developments of New Right thinking and at another level, the process of ageing in the British capitalist system and the State's concept of care. Examining the nature of care for black elders exposes the quality and scale of service delivery for *all* elders in general. This should therefore yield

Table 1.3: *Population by ethnic group and age 1984-86*

| Ethnic group | Percentage in each age group | | | | | Percentages and thousands | | |
	0-15	16-29	30-44	45-59	60 or over	Total¹ all ages (= 100%) (thousands)	Percentage UK-born	Percentage resident in English metropolitan areas
White	20	22	20	17	21	51,107	96	31
All ethnic minorities	34	28	20	13	4	2,432	43	69
of which								
West Indian or Guyanese	26	33	16	19	6	534	53	81
Indian	32	27	23	13	5	760	36	66
Pakistani	44	24	17	12	2	397	42	66
Bangladeshi	50	20	14	15	1	103	31	79
Chinese	28	28	28	11	5	115	24	52
African	26	31	27	12	4	103	35	75
Arab	17	40	28	10	5	66	11	62
Mixed	53	27	11	7	3	235	74	58
Other	28	25	30	12	4	119	28	63
Not stated	29	24	18	13	17	691	68	37
All ethnic groups	21	22	20	17	20	54,230	93	33

1. Population in private households.
Source: *Social Trends 18, 1988.*

important principles for SSDs, policy makers and social workers. We often talk about the economic crisis, the much heralded PSBR (Public Sector Borrowing Requirement) and its reduction in the pursuit of monetarist supply-side goals. These impact heavily on the provision of services for the elders. But, just as the thinking on economic crisis has changed its contours in the last decade, so too has the expression of racism. The effects of racism have become pernicious and deep within a climate in which prominent writers deny that racism exists (claims made by Honeyford, Flew et al). The case for a change and an expansion of service delivery to the black elders remains an urgent issue to be tackled now. We elaborate the principles, not recommendations, for such a case in Chapter 6.

2. Black elders in a historical context

Migration and settlement

Historical and social factors have determined the economic and social welfare position of the black elderly in Britain. These have affected them as a group throughout the process of migration, settlement and struggle against racism. The position of black elders cannot be seriously understood without looking at the political economy of black labour in Britain. This chapter summarises the historical and structural background which determines black elders' position in Britain today, with particular emphasis on consequent issues such as the type of employment, income and housing provision.

Migration in search of work, is not a new phenomenon: the labour market is the largest international market of all, drawing approximately fifty million people *directly* around the globe, trading their labour power in the international auction in labour. Walvin stresses the importance of such trade in *Passage to Britain* (1976):

> "Without immigration, London's population would in the pre-modern world, have collapsed, through the ravages of the City's heavy death rates".

Here the immigrants to London were the Scots and the Irish in the 16th, 17th and 18th centuries and the Jews, the Poles and other minority groups in the late 19th and 20th Century. Similarly, the black presence in Britain is not a recent phenomenon either: black people have been in Britain for approximately 500 years with many settling permanently — File and Power (1981); Fry (1983); Visram (1986). However, post-war migration to Britain from the Caribbean is often dated from the arrival of the *SS Empire Windrush* in 1948. As Hall (1988) remarks:

> "The history of the black diaspora in Britain begins here . . . what they were coming to was certainly not a 'Mother Country', a land of milk and honey, where the streets were paved with gold. Those who had served in His Majesty's Forces knew better than that. But, though the path for black men and women was

uncertain, there were opportunities, life-chances — chances to be taken by those who were willing to gamble with the future because they had so much at stake and so little to lose".

But the real beneficiary was the British economy itself: with the domestic economy expanding (as in Europe) and surplus labour in the colonies, importation of such labour met the needs of capital perfectly. The flow of black labour was self-regulating as Ceri Peach (1968) showed: the following table is adapted from his work (as cited in the Open University Unit, p.27).

Table 2.1: *Employment and Immigration 1956-60*

Year	Demand for Labour[1]	Arrivals from W. Indies	% Male[2]
1956	934,111	26,441	88.1
1957	725,271	22,473	52.7
1958	535,186	16,511	46.4
1959	653,120	20,397	49.3
1960	848,542	45,706	57.3

1. Average number of job vacancies, Ministry of Labour figures.
2. Migrant Services Division figures.

The data above clearly demonstrates the positive correlation between the demand for labour and the number of black migrants. Moreover, the responsiveness to changes in labour demand can be observed by examining proportionate changes for men arriving in Britain. The figures show that the proportionate change for male migrants is greater than the change in the demand for labour. The flow of black labour was not solely determined by the operation of the "invisible hand" (ie forces of demand and supply), but by active participation (to a smaller extent) of the State, in direct recruitment practices (London Transport, the British Hotels and Restaurants Association, not to forget Enoch Powell who as a Health Minister openly welcomed Caribbean nurses!). By 1958, there were approximately 125,000 Caribbeans and 58,000 Indians and Pakistanis. The 1948 Nationality Act had granted UK citizenship to all members of Britain's colonies and rights to enter and work to its ex-colonies' members. To this extent, the state had to contend with black labour and their families settling in Britain, whether the economy boomed or slumped, though it moved gradually towards the European system of contract labour through the operation of racist immigration Acts. So black migration in Britain was not migrant in the sense of a transitory, temporary nature but settler in the sense of exercising their legal rights of settlement. However, black migrants' initial desire to return "home with sufficient income", was altered by the first Commonwealth Immigrants Act of 1962, with the effect of

10

encouraging a "rush to bring families", as the right to remain in Britain became uncertain.

Employment

The "invisible hand" determined the size of the flow — the numbers — but the nature of employment was determined by full employment conditions and discrimination. The full employment situation ensured that existing workers could (and did) move out of the least desirable jobs to desirable ones with better pay and conditions. Black labour became "replacement labour", filling the gaps in key areas such as agriculture, brick-making, textiles, iron foundries in the manufacturing sector and several other (eg Transport and NHS) in the services sector. The following Table 2.2 shows the unequal distribution of black workers by sector and industry. This is because labour shortages were uneven and because of discrimination by employers and unions. Duffield, (1987) showed that the concentration of black workers in the Foundry Industry was determined by the trade union organisation. The PEP Report (Smith, 1977), also showed the concentration of night shift work amongst black workers. In Cohen and Jenner's study of the wool industry, in eight cases the companies stated that the reason they first employed Pakistani workers was closely associated with new capital investment that involved either shift work or very long hours.

Earnings

A further disparity exists in earning power. The PEP Report found wide differentials in earnings after allowing for age differences. "In the case of non-manual workers, earnings for white workers were £52.4 compared to £40.5 for black workers; for skilled manual workers earnings for white workers were £39.3 compared with £35.6 for black workers; while earnings of semi-skilled and unskilled manual workers are exactly the same. Moreover, there is a greater range of earnings at different job levels among white workers than among the minorities". The survey also found that black men were able to achieve equality of earnings with white men, but only when shift work was included. McNabb and Psacharopoulos (1981) using the results of General Household Survey data on average annual earnings also found differentials in earnings: white workers in 1972 had annual average earnings of £1519; black workers had £1294 — a difference of £225 which is significant at 1 per cent level.

This earnings disparity in the "working-period" directly accounts for differences in pensionable income. As Table 2.2 shows, black workers were

Table 2.2: *"Immigrant" workers as a percentage of the total workforce by industry*

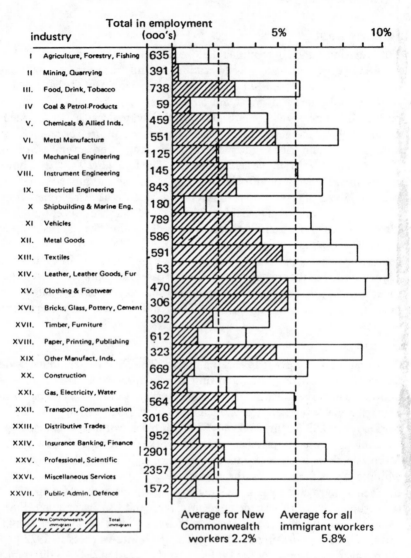

Source: *Runnymede Trust, 1980.*

highly represented in semi-skilled and unskilled manual jobs paying low wages and yielding lower pensions compared to workers in the professional, technical and management fields. The elders as a group on *fixed income* are vulnerable to a poor quality of life if we take the common standard of living variables. Black elders' material situation is further compounded by the following circumstances.

— The National Insurance Contributions made during the working period determines the level of pensionable income. Black elders arriving as post-war immigrants will not have a sufficient number of working years in Britain. With this partial state pension, "about a quarter of pensioned households in each ethnic group claim supplementary pension" (*PSI Survey* 1984).

— Occupational Pensions (superannuation schemes) are not uniform in all occupations and sectors. Barker (1983) explains that Afro-Caribbean elders receive higher pensions than Asians because working in the public sector resulted in contributions being paid on a regular basis. But Grant (1988) says that Caribbean women "were informed in the early years, not to pay the full graduated pension contribution" resulting in greater economic dependancy on their husbands. Many black elders have not worked in paid employment and therefore do not receive a pension. The Leicester Survey (1986) illustrates the extent of long-term unemployment experienced by black elders: in a sample of 109 Afro-Caribbean elders, it was found that 28 per cent were unemployed for one year or more; 13 per cent for two to six years and 9 per cent for eight to fifteen years between the age of fifty and retirement.

In Leicester itself the unemployment rates for 60-64 year group, within the "white" groups, was 19.6 per cent compared to 54.3 per cent for "Asians" and 55.4 per cent for "West Indians". Given that black elders occupied a particular position in the labour market (Table 2.2) with a higher propensity for structural change resulting in unemployment and redundancies (and some leaving because of ill-health — 27 per cent in the Leicester Survey), the potential to save for "old-age" is minimal or negative. This trend is likely to continue in the future since various studies point to the high rates of unemployment experienced by black men and women.

— Elders who came to Britain as "dependants" to join their families are not entitled to state income benefits. They are, therefore, economically dependent on their children or husbands.

To conclude, current low income and little (or no) previous savings, results

13

in hardship and subsistence living for many black elders. In a Breadline Survey in Greenwich (1985) 15 per cent of white elders interviewed said they were worried about having insufficient amounts of money for day-to-day living compared to 50 per cent of black elders. Black elders' poverty is further compounded by a failure to claim welfare benefits such as heating allowance or single payments for essential clothing.

Housing

Ensuring a steady stream of labour from the empire to fuel Britain's expansion was in the interest of the State and employers — providing housing and social amenities were clearly not. Eligibility requirements prevented black workers gaining access to council accommodation initially; only the Private Renting Sector provided an entry offering often poor accommodation with insecure tenancy agreements and exhorbitant rents. Owner-occupancy was a real alternative for many but those with little savings could afford only cheap houses in decaying areas. Employment patterns generally determined the broad patterns of settlement, close to the industrial conurbations chiefly in London, the North West, South and West Yorkshire, East and West Midlands. The PSI Survey (1984) summarises this situation:

> ". . . it should be remembered that just as the jobs that were available to black people were those not wanted by white people, so the areas in which black people worked and lived tended to be those that white people were already moving away from".

Black elders today are, therefore, settled in the inner city areas where jobs were available during their working-age. "It is estimated that 80 per cent of black people are concentrated in just 10 per cent of the census enumeration districts and that these are areas of poor housing, poor medical amenities and services" (Grant 1988). Due to this concentration mainly in urban settings, social service planners can easily determine the scale, nature and type of service provision for black elders. Whether the social services departments have been swift to respond to this or not will be examined in Chapter 3.

Conclusion

For the economy at large, black labour was cheap labour: since it was of working-age, there were no social capital costs involved, nor training costs. As Sivanandan (1982) comments:

> ". . . in the early years of migration, the 'coloured' worker came to Britain as a single man — as a unit of labour — unaccompanied by his family (which) meant

14

an additional saving to the country in terms of social capital: schools, housing, hospitals, transport and other infra-structural facilities. A fraction of the saving made from the import of these ready-made workers — let alone their active contribution in labour and taxes — could have served to increase social stock and improve social conditions if the Government had so willed. But capital and the state were concerned with the maximisation of profit, not with the alleviation of social need".

The brief examination of employment, concerning earning power and housing, above, locates the position of black elders in the context of migration and settlement. This impacts directly on their income power today and the consequent quality of life, with housing as an important factor. In the next chapter we examine the quality of care provided by social services departments in relation to the black elders.

3. Who cares for the black elders?

We have examined the demographic trends and socio-economic and historical characteristics of migration and "racial" status which have determined the quality of life of black elders today. This chapter focuses critically on key areas of services provided by the Social Services Departments (SSDs) to see how far they meet black elders' needs.

There are many potential problems in focusing on the existing services for the elders and then assessing whether black elders have effective access to these services. It can imply that existing services are satisfactory and appropriate, which may not be the case. We also risk labelling black elders as needy or dependant by virtue of their age, rather than because of personal necessity, racism and/or socio-economic and health status (some of which may be accentuated by the experience of ageing). As Muir Gray (quoted in Norton et al, 1986, p.52) states:

> "Many of the problems that occur more commonly in old age are not due to the ageing process itself, but to three other important processes: disease, loss of fitness and social consequences of growing old".

Further, like white elders, black elders are not a homogeneous group requiring *all* forms of social provision. They too belong to different income bands, experience different housing conditions and display various degrees of psychological and physical well-being across "ethnic groups", class, gender and generational divides. The degree of care required, therefore, depends on their social experience throughout life. Nevertheless, as we saw earlier, most black elders occupy a working-class position and experience poor financial, housing and health conditions. But they are neither passive nor powerless. Many will have been involved in the earlier campaigns of "the right to stay in Britain" or "campaigns against sin-bins or ESN placements", and fought against the fascists and the racists on "English" streets in the '50s and '60s. They may have also been involved in the struggles for self-determination on the international front (eg the inderpendence movements), as well as the daily struggles of bringing up

16

children and keeping families intact amid growing hostility in this country (Institute of Race Relations, 1987). The black elders of today were part of this resistance and hence their resistance to racism and exploitation in old age is not new. Portraying it as new plays into the hands of opponents who divide black generations into "passive" and "active" categories, seeing older people as passive and content to accept their position in British society, while black youth are viewed as suffering from "culture-clash", alienated and therefore in need of pacification by the State (John, 1978).

It is in this context that we must address the issue of black elders' entitlement and the extent to which they are receiving an equal share of services from the SSDs, as an agent of the Welfare State. We must also question whether the nature of service provision is appropriate to black elders' requirements.

Unlike education or health care which cater for the broad section of the population, "social services are there to help those that cannot entirely help themselves. Social services are all about the amelioration of the socially disadvantaged" (CRE, 1978). SSDs provide services for elders ranging from: Home Helps, Meals-on-Wheels, Luncheon Clubs, Day Centres to Sheltered Housing and Residential Homes. To provide and make use of these services, it is assumed that consumers have the necessary information, can translate their need into a demand, and ensure that they find the service satisfactory. To explore this premise, we will consider various empirical studies conducted in the last decade. Throughout this study we refer to these studies in various areas of service provision. Table 3.1 identifies these key surveys and their respective sample size.

Table 3.1: *Key studies of black elders 1981-1987*

Area of survey	Year	Sample size	Sample groups
1. AFFOR study in Birmingham by Bhalla, A, & Blakemore, K,	1981	400 (179;169;52)	Afro-Caribbeans, Asians & Europeans.
2. Nottingham by Berry, S, et al	1981	148	Afro-Caribbeans.
3. Age Concern Research Unit in Manchester & London by Barker, J,	1984	619 (234;370;15)	Afro-Caribbeans, Asians, Africans.
4. Greenwich by Turnbull, A,	1985	27 (4;23)	Afro-Caribbeans, Asians.
5. Coventry by Holland, B, & Lewando-Hundt, G,	1986	1,234 (71;1,163)	Afro-Caribbeans, Asians.
6. Leicester by Farrah, M,	1987	109	Afro-Caribbeans.

We shall also refer to the findings of two other projects: (i) a report on a seminar "Elders in Ethnic Minorities" by Glendenning, F, (1979) and (ii) a SSI survey of three SSDs in London by Prime, R, (1987). In most surveys the sample group includes elders of 55 years of age and over.

Information or awareness of services

We first examine the issue of the extent to which information on services is provided by SSDs. Table 3.2 identifies the level of awareness of services across two different studies.

According to the Birmingham study, Europeans are most aware of the services available to them with Afro-Caribbeans also showing a high degree of awareness. This is confirmed by the Coventry study. Asians, however, have very limited awareness: in most cases (in both surveys) over 80 per cent of the Asian elders had no knowledge of services available to them, except Old Peoples' Homes (33 per cent Birmingham) and Day Centres (46 per cent Coventry). This is in comparison with Afro-Caribbeans, 80 per cent of whom were informed of services. Some black elders lack information not only on services, but also on financial benefits (eg additional heating allowance). As Chapter Two showed, their low income is partly due to a lack of knowledge on benefits which could supplement poor income. Many low-income groups, particularly older people, do not claim their full entitlements, partly because the welfare state is not efficient in providing information. However, as the Coventry and Leicester studies show, much could be achieved; even in the process of conducting research (eg through giving information on the type of services and making referrals to agencies).

In order to acquire information, communication skills are essential, that is, communication in English: information on the system of benefits and services is disseminated through a maze of leaflets and application forms. DHSS officers assume that the potential recipients speak English, can read and understand leaflets and fill in forms; assumptions which probably should not be made even for white clients! The Birmingham survey found that 88 per cent of Asian elders could not speak English, while the Age Concern Study showed a similar trend with "38 per cent Asians not being able to speak and write *any* English compared to 4 per cent Afro-Caribbeans" (p.23, my emphasis). The difficulties in communicating in English are not restricted to "Asian" or Afro-Caribbean elders: Ukranians and Poles (Jagucki, 1983); Cypriots (Norman, 1985) and Chinese (Lim, 1979; Lyn, 1982) also experience similar problems in communication. Clearly, communication is a pre-requisite to gaining access to services of the Welfare State and an inability to communicate in English disadvantages

Table 3.2: *Knowledge of services by 'ethnic' group* (%)

SERVICES (Birmingham Study 1981)	Afro-Caribbeans (%)	Asians (%)	Europeans (%)
1. Old peoples' homes	89	33	96
2. Home helps	83	19	94
3. Meals-on-wheels	80	13	96
4. Day centres	60	13	67
5. Luncheon clubs	36	5	42
6. Night watch	23	4	36
7. Home visiting service for old people	58	11	62
8. None of these	3	64	2

Source: *AFFOR, Birmingham Study 1981, p.28.*

SERVICES (Coventry Study 1986)	Afro-Caribbeans (%)	Asians (%)
1. Residential homes	87	7
2. Home helps	86	16
3. Mobile meals	87	14
4. Day centres	94	46
5. Luncheon clubs	80	5
6. Sheltered housing	63	11

Source: *Coventry Study 1986, p.4 in Social Services Research (1987).*

19

recipients further. Increasingly, many SSDs have started to translate their leaflets into relevant community languages and a few provide an interpreting service. But is this sufficient to ensure a higher take-up of existing services by black elders?

Language is an important factor in acquiring information, but does not determine the take-up of services. The premise that having sufficient information leads to a direct use of services can be tested by analysing the Coventry data further.

Table 3.3: *Use of services*

Services	Asians %	Afro-Caribbeans %
Mobile meals	0	0
Home helps	1	8
Sheltered housing	1	3
Day centres	4	32
Luncheon clubs	0	22
Residential homes	0	0

Source: *Coventry Study 1986, p.6 in Social Services Research (1987).*

If having sufficient information determined service take-up, we would expect to find an acceptance-rate around 80 per cent for Afro-Caribbeans (based on Table 3.2). The above data shows this is not the case. The premise is also refuted by other studies, for example, the Nottingham Study (1981).

Table 3.4 *Rejection of services by Afro-Caribbean elders*

Services	Rejection rate %	(Use of service %)[1]
Home helps	17	(83)
Meals-on-wheels	72	(28)
Luncheon clubs	70	(30)
Day centres	53	(47)
Homes for the elderly	84	(16)

1. Derived from the rejection rate. Author's modification.
Source: *Quoted in Glendenning & Pearson 1988 p.15.*

In both studies, the use of day centres and home helps is higher than other services (though the use of luncheon clubs is greater than home helps in the Coventry study). Does greater knowledge of day centres, for example, account for its higher usage? Unfortunately, the data in both surveys is inadequate in this regard. However, we can assume that the basis for rejection of services is possibly due to factors other than the level of awareness, in the Nottingham study. We will later explore the reasons for such variation when examining the specific issues of day centres and home helps.

The disparity between knowing what is available and the low take-up of services, particularly for the Afro-Caribbean groups requires further investigation. One SSD Director is quoted as saying:

> "The area of concern is that many basic services provided by the Department appear to be undermined by minority ethnic groups . . . The issue is a very serious one requiring further work and it is recognised that simple solutions are unlikely to be found". (Greenwich 1985, p.33).

We next focus on specific services to understand black elders' perceptions of each type of service and reasons for their low take-up.

Services

Domiciliary Services

The Chronically Sick and Disabled Persons Act 1970, section 2(i) allows for domiciliary services and mobile meals provision. Domiciliary services also incorporate home helps and home care services. These services largely reflect the needs of elders who have no family, relatives or friends to turn to for support. The Birmingham Survey found that for Europeans 19 per cent received home help and 6 per cent mobile meals compared to 9 per cent and 2 per cent respectively for Afro-Caribbeans. Asians did not receive either home help or mobile meals services, though *only 33 per cent* of the Asians expressed no interest in these services on the grounds that their family and relatives would provide care for them.

In a study of *West Indian Elderly in Leicester* (1977), Jo Cooper cites a case of a black woman in poor health, with no relatives, who required practical help (eg shopping). She was entitled to home help but was unaware of her rights; young black individuals with whom she spoke were similarly unaware. This shows that language is not the only barrier faced by the elders.

Home helps cover a wide range of caring activities, though personal care is regarded as a priority over, for example, domestic tasks. Hence a report by Hertfordshire SSD states

> "Much more may now be demanded (of a home help) in the way of forming a relationship with an old person, working with her, teaching a little, stimulating a little, offering advice on buying or the storing of food, detecting urgent problems of deterioration and so on". (Cited in Norton et al 1986 p.121).

These surveys do not explain the higher incidence of use of home helps, particularly for the Afro-Caribbeans, by people who are *aware* of this service (Table 3.3 and 3.4). One may, therefore, suggest that as the home help service is provided at the clients' home, this offers a certain degree of autonomy. The tasks performed may be negotiated through establishing personal relationships. There may also be a higher number of black staff employed as home helps, though without such data, we can only speculate.

Meals account for less than 2 per cent of total gross expenditure by SSDs and are provided through mobile meals, luncheon clubs and day centres. The questions of food in terms of content/type (vegetarian, halal, etc), methods of preparation, styles of cooking and the standard of hygiene (Cooper 1977) are the first and foremost issues raised by respondents in all the surveys and many articles. This is not surprising as food is a basic necessity and is central to many peoples' source of beliefs and identity. But, the element of surprise still continues to be displayed (Greenwich 1985, p.38):

> "It was estimated in February 1983, that slightly less than 5 per cent of Greenwich's elderly population received either meals-on-wheels or a lunch club meal each day from Monday to Friday from the Department's Catering Section. Applying this percentage to the NCWP elderly population, it would be expected that 28 black pensioners might avail themselves of this service. Yet there appears to be **little or no take-up by them of the traditional British foods offered**". (My emphasis.)

The question "what is wrong with the ordinary meals-on-wheels services?" continually recurrs from SSDs throughout the country. And yet this one meal can be crucial for many black elders, as it is for white elders. We considered earlier the main reasons for low pensionable income for black elders and in response to the question of payment difficulties — one in four black persons said that they had *difficulty in affording food* (Leicester survey 1987). When many black elders are simply subsisting, mobile meals is not an option but a necessity, an essential lifeline. Meanwhile, many authorities cater for "special meals" based on health and dietary requirements (eg diabetes). Looking to luncheon clubs, a similar trend to mobile meals emerges for black elders. The importance of luncheon clubs is best summarised by the following:

> "Luncheon clubs are a part of the community system enabling the elderly or the infirm to maintain an independent pattern of life for as long as possible by providing motivation for them to leave their homes and opportunities to meet other people, to enjoy social functions, to participate in the running of the club itself and to receive advice and practical assistance as necessary around a focal point of a nourishing meal". (Wiltshire County Council SSD Review Group Paper for meals-on-wheels and luncheon clubs, December 1978, quoted in Norton et al 1986).

Thus luncheon clubs play an important role in alleviating isolation and depression and raising self-esteem and morale. With a few exceptions in the statutory sector (eg Brent Asian Meals Service where meals for Hindus and Muslims are cooked by the elders and deliveries are made to those house-bound [Norman, 1985]), the type of food and social activities remain ethnocentric. Increasingly, luncheon clubs, mobile meals services are being set up by the black voluntary sector: self-help schemes which are innovative, meeting some needs of black elders and at a low cost. This will be considered further in Chapter 6.

Day Centres

Day Centres stand in-between institutional care and domiciliary services. They are seen as providing social and recreational facilities and offering an opportunity for social contact using other local authority services eg adult education, library and recreation (Leisure) services. Those who require greater physical care such as after-care post-hospitalisation, or a substitute for a residential home, would receive attention from the health services.

The Birmingham survey found that 4 per cent of Afro-Caribbeans and 2 per cent of Asians attended day centres compared to 6 per cent of Europeans. However, 64 per cent of Afro-Caribbeans and 35 per cent of Asians said they would attend a day centre if one was near home compared to 31 per cent of Europeans. The ease of getting to a day centre then is a significant factor with a clear need for community transport facilitating access. The survey also revealed the following reasons given by black elders for not using day centre facilities:

— concern over speaking and understanding English;
— concern over the type of food offered and the catering arrangements;
— inability to participate fully in leisure pursuits because of health/physical reasons.

Two further reasons could be added to this:

— Black elders were subjected to racist abuse and experienced hostility from the white elders at day centres;
— there was little to share and exchange with white elders (eg the leisure and educational facilities were inappropriate); and the "feelings of being the only black person around" clearly made establishing relationships difficult.

This lack of commonality is expressed quite clearly by one black elder:

"At the moment I go to the day centre, but I would like to go somewhere with more retired West Indians. We could talk, and we understand each other, and we could help one another". (Quoted in Glendenning & Parsons, 1988, p.40).

Some SSDs are beginning to open up day centre facilities, usually for one or two days a week, specifically for Asians, Afro-Caribbean, Chinese or Cypriot elders. Patel stresses the importance of such a facility and its effect on black elders, examining a case of a black elder, Mr Singh, who had lost the will to survive and lived alone with no family in Britain. His life was radically altered when he agreed to attend a day centre once a week when it was open specifically to Asian groups.

> "Mr Singh started attending the day centre every Tuesday; this was the one day of the week he really began to enjoy. It became a great ritual to him . . . Attending the day centre began to have a social significance for him". (Patel, H. *Community Care* June 5, 1986).

Day centres then offer not only a meeting place for social facility, but through various activities, if appropriate, can provide an intellectual and recreational stimulus for elders in need. Black elders too suffer from loneliness and social isolation compounded by the added effects of racism.

On the question of social contacts, the Birmingham Survey noted that 83 per cent of Asian men and 35 per cent of women go out daily (and the proportion does not decline with age). The ratio is 59 per cent of Afro-Caribbean men and 40 per cent women; and 82 per cent of European men and 60 per cent of women go out daily. This indicates their relative levels of mobility and the potential usage of services, particularly of men. Although going out daily may result in contacts with relatives, friends, state agency staff or visits to shops, there is no qualitative measure of social contact itself (the survey authors acknowledge this), so frequency of trips and encounters with different individuals, albeit important, are equated with the differential nature of social encounters — exchanging a hello with a friend is on a par with a conversation with another! What is, however, significant are the number of black elders who have no daily contact with friends, relatives or "caring" staff: 6.7 per cent Afro-Caribbeans, 13 per cent Asians; 44 per cent Europeans. Thus, a significant number of elders are socially isolated. This accords with the Derby study (1986) which highlighted the problems of those black elders, Pakistanis particularly, who live alone. For many, the immigration laws have ensured that their families remain divided. A similar fate awaits many Bangladeshi men as they grow old in coming years and attempt to unite with their families.[1]

---

1. We are already witnessing the operation of racism when families attempt to unite, with the recent case of Bangladeshi families and Tower Hamlets Council. Housing provision is here refused on the grounds that "they made themselves intentionally homeless by leaving their homes in Bangladesh"!

As day centres also cater for those elders who require some form of health assistance, we need to briefly examine the common problems reported by black elders. Table 3.5 summarises the findings of the Birmingham (1981) and Leicester (1986) surveys.

Table 3.5: *Health problems reported by the elders, by 'ethnic' group (%)*

	Afro-Caribbean		Asian Birmingham Only	European Birmingham Only
Problem	*Birmingham* % (N = 179)	*Leicester* % (N = 109)	% (N = 169)	% (N = 52)
1. Sight	61	89	53	52
2. Feet/walking	50	28	36	48
3. Hearing	7	12	22	31
4. Dental	15	30	21	10
5. Depression	n.a.	26	n.a.	n.a.
6. Forgetfulness	n.a.	34	n.a.	n.a.

It is clear that a great number of ailments distress elders from all communities. Along with isolation, disillusionment and other problems, poor health is clearly something which could be treated at day and health centres and a critical justification for such establishments. Adequate transportation to these centres is obviously needed, particularly since many ailments (sight, feet/walking problems) directly affect mobility. This issue is even more important for black elders because of linguistic difficulties and racial harassment en route. Community transportation would ameliorate some of these difficulties. The various problems discussed in this section indicates a clear demand for day centre provisions by the black elders.

Sheltered Housing

Local Authorities under the National Assistance Act, 1948 Section 21, are responsible for providing:

"Suitable accommodation for all who through age, infirmity, or for any other reason are in need of care and attention not otherwise available". (Quoted in a SCEMSC Report p.11).

It is estimated that around 10 per cent of elders live in sheltered/residential/hospital accommodation. They may live in:

CATEGORY 1: Self-contained housing for one or two "active" persons (perhaps with communal facilities).

CATEGORY 2: Flats with common area and communal facilities, together with a warden accommodation.

PART III Residential Care: This represents care for the very elderly who require continuous aid with daily tasks as a result of severe physical and mental infirmity.

According to the Age Concern Working Party Report (1984) the objective of sheltered housing is to:

> "provide housing which is designed primarily to meet the likely future needs of elderly people after they give up an active working life, in order to enable them to live independently at home until they die, bearing in mind that the minority will present problems associated with fraility in old age, eg falling, incontinence, confusion, depression and immobility". (Quoted in Norton et al 1986).

However, Table 3.2 showed that in Coventry no Asian or Afro-Caribbean respondents were using residential homes, while only 1 per cent and 3 per cent respectively used sheltered housing. SCEMSC offers us a variety of reasons for such a low usage, including: lack of information, particularly for Asians (see also Table 3.1); care is provided by the family instead; rejection of the concept of residential or sheltered housing ("I would rather die first than go into one", Leicester Survey, 1987); and inappropriate staff and services. Black elders, however, may not be against such accommodation in principle. The Leicester survey asked respondents what type of accommodation they would choose if they were unable to care for themselves. Three (2.8 per cent) out of 109 persons stated that they would prefer older person's homes; 57 (52.3 per cent) referred to Warden-assisted housing; 17 (15.6 per cent) indicated a wish for church-provided accommodation; and 21 (19.3 per cent) stated that they preferred to remain in their own homes with external assistance being provided. Eleven people (10.1 per cent) were undecided. The fact that over 50 per cent preferred sheltered Warden-assisted housing is significant in underlining black elders' needs and potential demands for housing provided by the welfare state. If the objective as stated by Age Concern is to be met, then consideration of home location, composition of staff and residents, appropriate food, language and religious practices, together with a firm commitment to counter racism, are important factors to be addressed when planning housing provision for black elders.

The type of accommodation offered to black clients is also an important consideration. The assessment form should be the best guide in determining the type of housing granted to the client. However, SCEMSC alerts us to questions of participation "to what extent is the older client today involved in an interview . . . increasingly, decisions are taken on their behalf without their knowledge by their relatives irrespective of whether the elders are themselves able to make decisions" because of:

26

> "(a) pressure on the relatives to relieve themselves of the responsibility to care;
> (b) overcrowded accommodation;
> (c) a young family (children taking priority);
> (d) lack of such support networks as an extended family or other relief carers via a neighbourhood or other such scheme;
> (e) ignorance of the services available/provisions made through the Local Authority". (SCEMSC Report p.19).

So, not only must black elders contend with inappropriate housing provision, but they must also demand the right of having a choice in the matter! Apparently, in the majority of cases, when homes are offered, no adjustments or changes are made to the "normal" provision, thereby retaining the character of sheltered and residential accommodation as white-centered and white-dominated. The following two examples from the Birmingham survey encapsulate SSDs' general view towards creating suitable forms of housing for black elders.

> In one home although there were no black residents, the home had provided temporary accommodation to an Asian woman for six weeks while her family left her for a holiday. "When asked if they had provided for any special needs, the reply was that it would have been unfair to other residents if this lady was given special treatment. It was seen as difficult for the home to change its routine for one resident". (p.36)

> In a second case concerning two Afro-Caribbean men in one home and a woman in another, "staff said that they presented no problems to the homes and were culturally well adjusted to the 'British way of life'." (p.36).[1]

It appears that if black elders can culturally assimilate, then the practices in sheltered or residential housing can continue to function as always! However, should black elders' requirements, which in most cases will not fit the (perceived) norm of "a British way of life", be regarded as "special", problematic or even deviant? Is it just culturally appropriate services that black elders demand? Although there is scant direct mention of racism in most of the surveys considered, the many views of black elders suggest that their expectations and demands go beyond providing "ethnically sensitive or culturally appropriate" services.

Conclusion

Black elders clearly have a demand for services which SSDs provide, with the qualification that these services must change to reflect their practices,

---

1. The family and the elders may wish to live in one household. Changing the housing situation for the elder alone may not be the best response in this event. When the housing situation for the entire family is poor, remedying the family housing condition may be the best solution in the context of care.

Graph 3.1a: *Black elders' usage of services (Coventry Study [1986])*
(Percentage of elders using or willing to use a service)

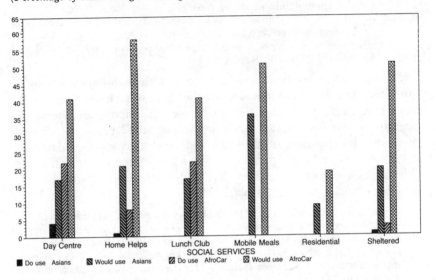

Graph 3.1b: *Black elders' usage of services (Leeds Study [1986])*
(Percentage of elders using or willing to use a service)

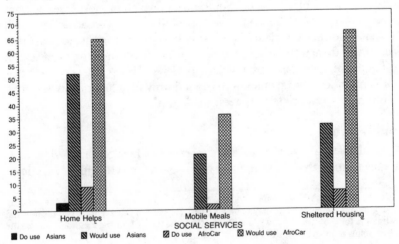

beliefs and choices. We have already seen under specific provisions, the need by black elders to use such services. Graph 3.1 aptly summarises what the demand for various services might be if there was sufficient awareness and they were adapted to meet black elders' needs.

Although we have two different sample sizes in each survey (and possibly differences in intended usage for this and other reasons) it is irrefutable that black elders have clearly indicated their potential demand for services. We investigate this further in the next chapter.

4. The invisibility factor — SSDs' response to black elders

The empirical evidence discussed in Chapter 3 has illustrated the needs of black elders in Britain. It has also shown that black elders are severely under-represented in all the services provided by the statutory sector: the SSDs. We have also seen that if there was sufficient knowledge of services provided, and if these were deemed appropriate to their requirements, they would be used by black elders — (Graph 3.1). What then prevents SSDs from making the necessary changes to which the black elders, thus far neglected, are entitled to? In this chapter we look at how black elders have been rendered invisible through the acceptance of a myth on the role of the black family and record the nature of SSDs' response over the last decade.

The myth — "they look after their own"

The popular image of a white British family whether projected on a cereal packet or in family planning advertisements is a husband, wife and two children. For a black family (irrespective of "ethnicity") the popular image is one of an extended family network, "families within families", providers of care and social and psychological support. Strangely such virtues are married to a conception of "overcrowded households"! The former image of a nuclear family as a representative family structure in Britain is fast diminishing (*Social Trends* 1988). However, the latter image of an extended family and its role continues to thrive among service providers and the wider society despite the facts.

> "Overall, the proportion of extended families living together is 21 per cent — higher than among other groups, but not the norm". (Westwood & Bachu, 1988, commenting on Asian families).

Black elders are not homogeneous in their family and household patterns as shown by Table 4.1. Although the Afro-Caribbean households display similar patterns to Europeans (Birmingham survey), the number of black elders in Afro-Caribbean and Asian Groups living alone and/or with 'one other' is indicative of the decline of extended families. However, the prevalence of Asian elders living in extended family structures may be better attributed to economic circumstances rather than just customs and traditions. More importantly, the household composition data obfuscates the question of care: for example, the fact that a higher number of Asian elders live in an extended family does not necessarily mean that their material and psychological needs are provided by the family. Nor should we assume that those living alone are permanently isolated from their family, relatives and friends. Family structures do not remain static over time and black families are not an exception; changes are continually taking place as they adjust and adapt to internal and external conditions. SCEMSC (1986) provides us with an important view of an Afro-Caribbean Elders Group at Lambeth:

> "who felt that the extended family link . . . is not taken seriously by their children . . . felt that their family life was qualitatively lacking, but did not want to 'blame' their children for what they saw as an environment problem". (Cited in Glendenning and Pearson 1988, p.27).

For those elders who came to Britain as "dependants" to join their children (or husband), an absence of roles, the impact of new ways and values (particularly at a time when due to ageing, changes may be more difficult to accept) and the frequent inability to speak English leaves them isolated and disillusioned, with little potential to lead a productive life. They also face poverty. As "dependants" or "sponsored immigrants" they are not entitled to state income and so are financially dependant on their children. The unity of the family for many elders is achieved at a substantial personal, social and economic cost. Their needs, therefore, are acute and urgent.

We also considered in Chapter 3 that some black elders not only live alone but have no family in Britain, thus the statement "they look after their own" is inapplicable to this group.

There is sufficient evidence that the extended family structure is declining. Even if this were not so, we should not assume that the elders' needs are catered for in the extended family. Hence, "they care for their own" is a myth, a serious one at that because it is used as a buffer by the SSDs against making any necessary changes to the existing services and expanding the level of service provision. The important question here is not whether extended family structures exist, but whether black elders are receiving different forms of care from the welfare state, according to their requirements, irrespective of the nature of the family structure. The maintenance and the reproduction of the myth that "they look after their

Table 4.1: *Household composition by 'ethnic' group from three surveys (%)*

a. Birmingham Survey (1981):

Group	1-3 (%)	4-8 (%)	9+ (%)
Afro-Caribbeans	85	12	3
Asians	20	56	14
Europeans	96	2	2

b. Age Concern Survey (1984):

Group	Live alone (%)	Live with only 1 other (%)	Live with 6 others (%)
Afro-Caribbeans	36	32	2
Asians	5	13	71

c. Coventry Survey (1986):

Group	Alone (%)	Spouse only (%)	Spouse + relatives (%)	In-Laws (%)	Close relatives (%)	Other (%)
Afro-Caribbeans	17	35	35	3	10	Nil for spouse & friends/friends-institutions.
Asians	3	16	66	12	2	

own" has allowed the SSDs to evade their responsibility of providing care — a cost-effective evasion because it saves resources; does not require a change in the pattern of resource distribution; and keeps the existing services intact (thereby eliminating restructuring/administrative costs). Nevertheless, the family is generally viewed as an important institution, particularly at a time when the state, with its supply-side, monetarist orientation, is marketing (and quite successfully regarding the growth of private sector care) the concept of voluntarism and family care as "freedom of choice", in contradistinction to state care. We will explore this further in Chapter 6. The importance of the family as a social institution will be briefly considered in our understanding of internal colonialism in the next chapter. Suffice it to say, many so-called third-world economies are certainly not suffering from the illusion "they care for their own". Bal Chauhan, at a conference on black elders was recently cited as saying:

"Agencies in urban areas in India and Pakistan had started to address the need for residential care for elderly people, while there was still an assumption in this country that Asian families will always care for their own". (Jolley, M, 1988).

It is not the black family who should be examined, but the racism of SSDs in their continued failure to provide care. In 1974 Lees and Gardiner (Age Concern Manifesto) stated: "At the moment the elderly remain a hidden problem. Few recognise their existence and when they are seen, it tends to be assumed that they are cared for by their families and are not the responsibility of the local authority".

Three years later, a CRC Report (1977) said "it was very rare for social services committees to have even discussed the needs of minorities".

This led the ADSS in their report (1978) to summarise the progress of social services as: "patchy, piecemeal and lacking in strategy".

Ten years on, policy making on anti-racism consists of monitoring, Section 11 funding for specific posts, anti-racist training, day centres and luncheon club provision. These are often cited as a few changes which some SSDs have made with regard to black elders. However, a survey by the Social Services Inspectorate in 1985, which found that only one of seventeen SSDs in the North West England had a policy on anti-racism and ethnic minorities, is more typical. SSDs, with or without an anti-racist policy, must be assessed in relation to the changes made in services as required by clients. Chapter 3 illustrated a continuous trend of unmet needs of black elders in the '80s. It would, therefore, be safe to conclude that SSDs' progress today on black elders is uneven, be it in the "rich South" (for example, the SSI's survey of three London Boroughs illustrates the variations) or "poor North". In the '80s black elders may no longer be a "hidden problem" in many authorities, but the solution and changes remain invisible in most cases.[1]

To explain this trend of neglect let us look at the responses SSDs give when called to make the necessary changes to black elders' needs. They range from (i) "our service is open to all"; through (ii) "we do not discriminate against anyone", "providing for 'special' needs is discriminatory — it's racism in reverse", or "we can't do anything about racist abuse in the Centre — the old cannot be expected to change their ways"; to (iii) (from staff) "we are social workers — we can't be racist" (because the profession's ethos and practices are about care and helping the disadvantaged) or, at the other extreme, "we are all racists" — echoing the view of RAT ('race awareness training').

A response from one SSD, some twelve years ago, still retains an air of familiarity today when adequate and appropriate services for black elders are called for. In this particular case, the SSD had full knowledge of the different needs of Asian elders and refused to support an urban aid application on the following grounds:

> "It is so much harder for older people to accept different dietary provisions, different attitudes, to learn a new language. I think that to expect an old person to settle happily into one of our old people's homes or one of our luncheon clubs is asking an awful lot if they are not reasonably assimilated . . . We had a suggestion come up for Urban Aid from an Indian Association for a day centre for elderly Asians and the council could not back it, specifically on the grounds that they were not supporting any type of provision for one community, only things that were being provided for the residents no matter what their ethnic origin". (CRC 1976).

It follows from the above that the services are "open to all" and it is up to black elders to use them in their present form since to make changes would be discriminatory.

In the next chapter we will critically appraise the underlying reasons for SSDs' "colour-blind" response towards black elders and suggest a framework locating their response.

---

1. See the findings of the most recent survey in 116 SSDs conducted by the CRE, 1989, *Racial Equality in Social Services Departments*.

5. A conceptual framework for the analysis of British racism and its consequences, particularly at the organisational level

It is insufficient merely to describe the current state of social services provision to black elders. It is necessary to seek for an explanation of SSDs' continued failure to respond adequately to black elders' demands. Why is it that responses such as "we treat them all the same" or "they do not exist" (despite their changing articulation over time) continue to thrive and receive particular meanings in the planning and policy-making of SSDs? This chapter offers a conceptual framework for understanding and underpinning SSDs' responses. This framework is valid for a wide range of applications in anti-racist analyses and practices.

We begin by stating that racism can be regarded as a structural phenomenon, because of its historical roots and ideological conditions. We discussed some of the consequences — employment, low incomes and inadequate housing — when locating the structural position of black elders in Britain in Chapter 2.

Diagram 5.1 encapsulates an analysis of the main forms of racism and their consequences. The first segment of the diagram, "a partial socio-economic and ideological backdrop", identifies some of the many underlying factors which determine racism in Britain. Some of these have been mentioned earlier, and they have been extensively covered in the "race relations" literature — Cox (1949); Hall et al (1978); Hall (1980); Husband (1981); Miles (1982); Sivanandan (1976, 1982) and several resourceful publications from the Institute of Race Relations and the Runnymede Trust. Hall (1980) has provided a concise statement of the structuralist approach to understanding racism. He suggests it is necessary to identify specific economic, political and ideological practices and to understand how they interact within a particular social structure in its historical context. In a class-based society these practices will determine the position of different social groups in relation to the central economic and class structures that shape the society. Racism enters and operates both as an ideology and a set of practices. As an ideology it legitimates the positions ascribed to different groups. As a set of practices it helps to sustain the hierarchy of these groups. From this perspective, racism is fully integrated into the economic core of society and will inevitably interact with a range of cultural, political and ideological agendas in the society.

Individual racism

At one level this makes it necessary to consider how racism is articulated at the individual level, of social services staff, who *deliver* the services prescribed to black elders. Individual racism is however only one part of the broader equation of racism; it is part of the individual consciousness in the day-to-day functioning of the organisational objectives and is developed not as an innate part of "human nature", but a structural process of historical acts as implied by the first segment of our diagram. In other words, the material conditions make this (and other) forms of racism — individual racism — active and significant. So years of exploitation and racial subordination, justified by racist claims, (eg through the development of "scientific" theories of racial superiority or the new racism, based on sociobiology today) imprints heavily on people's consciousness: the individual sense of identity which is expressed in their "normal" behaviour and practice. Adopting a historical perspective on social identity and inter-group behaviour, Husband (1980) argues that,

> "We should anticipate that the emergence of a significant black population within Britain would stimulate culturally latent notions of white superiority and black inferiority. Indeed, throughout the 1960s we had ample demonstration of the definition of black persons as non-citizens, mere 'immigrants', and through the mass media there was created an ubiquitous acceptance that Britain has an 'immigration problem'."

So it is within the concept of "British identity" and "British culture" — chequered with racist ideology and liberalism — that white (and black) social service workers practice in relation to white and black clients. For black clients their daily experience structured by racism is omitted from the context of service provision. All clients are treated alike. Many a statement or principle echoes the sounds of equity and fairness, but is actually racism by default.

A case study of "Mr A", cited by Rooney (1987) illustrates the nature of individual racism and "benign" neglect. Mr A was moved to a home in the voluntary sector (Landseer) from a hospital, without his consent, as a result of a stroke. This presented a number of "ordinary problems" for the staff. Rooney cites various instances of how these "ordinary problems" were not solved in the context of care, because social workers' judgements were

Diagram 5.1: *A conceptual framework for the analysis of British racism and its consequences, particularly at the organisational level*

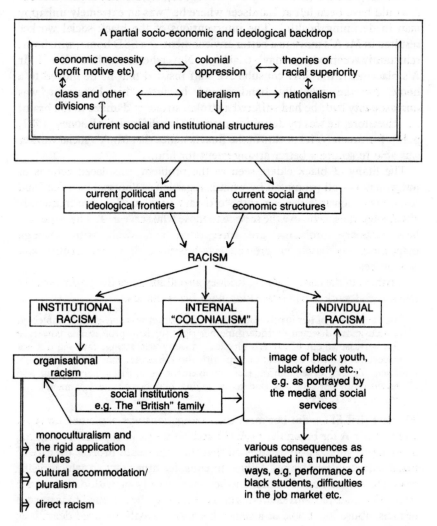

influenced by racist perceptions. Without the intervention of a black social worker from BSWP (Black Social Workers Project), Rooney argues that Mr A would have been left at Landseer where he "was an extremely unhappy man in declining health". The interventions of the black social worker resulted in Mr A's move to a better environment — a SSD home, which was reluctantly accepted, on a day's trial basis. Nevertheless, at the review of Mr A's placement, the SSD consultative staff insisted that he be moved to a home for the mentally handicapped because "his behaviour was unreasonably bad; he had suffered a stroke; stroke = damage to the brain; . . . therefore, he was by definition mentally handicapped" (Rooney, 1987, p.87). Fortunately, it appears in the final instance that Mr A's social worker was able to secure a better arrangement for him.[1]

The litany of black elders seen as the problem, misplaced actions or judgements — all prompted by what is regarded as "normal practice" and racist views towards dealing with "ordinary problems" — are frequently cited, from those who use the service to those who serve in it. The issue is of how ordinary problems are interpreted and dealt with through inappropriately based or pre-conceived notions of racial identity and stereotypes.

Further, in the case of Mr A, Rooney also illuminates the position of the black social worker when working with black clients.

> "In the process of her involvement the social worker was consistently subjected to accusations directed to undermine her right to claim professional power: ie that her assessment of Mr A's physical capacity was wrong, that she did not respect protocol in her relationship with the Landseer, that she insensitively raised Mr A's expectations. Her involvement as a Black person was also devalued in that she was said to be giving him favourable treatment . . ." (Rooney 1987, p.89).

The fact that SSDs did not meet their obligations was explained away by blaming Mr A for being the problem and his social worker for getting too involved! It should also be stressed that the assessment process for care of black elders suffers from a failure to consider other factors which result from the experience of racism in the wider society or within the service itself. For example, sufficient importance may not be attached to instances of racist abuse in a home or a centre because the staff involved deem it as

---

1. This case highlights the insidious nature of referrals and the role of influential sources (eg GPs) in the context of assessment and access to social service provision. The "influential professionals'" decision to refer black clients to a particular service (or not) is equally determined by general racist assumptions about black people/black family, as those held by social services staff.

insignificant or because white elders cannot be expected to change their behaviour! Hence black elders must put up with racism or not use the service.

But change has also taken place: the '80s has thus far witnessed a plethora of "race" training measures, recognising that there is a need to change attitudes; to inform and educate white workers in particular; and enable them to provide an adequate service delivery to black clients. There is consensus on the need to train social services staff to work in a pluralist society, ranging from SSDs, through writers such as Cheetham, Ahmed, Small et al, to CCETSW and SSI. However, there is no consensus on the training methods necessary to achieve this but many questions on racism abound. Should training be directed to giving information on cultures of "minority groups" or cultural information with current aspects of racism (immigration, employment etc) on the fringes? What perspective does the training take on racism? Is the approach anthropological, culturally pluralist or structuralist? Does the training on racism exist on the periphery or at the centre of *all* training? Whatever the nature of the questions, Racism Awareness Training (RAT) remains the most popular means of *taking action on racism today*. We are examining RAT in this section because of its stress on the role of the individual and personal psychology, ("change personal attitudes and the problem of racism is solved") a conception which is acceptable to social work because of its emphasis on individual casework. Just as RAT is becoming more acceptable (with some changes to its earlier variant originating from Judy Katz's work), so are the many critiques, in particular after Sivanandan's assault on RAT ("RAT and the Degradation of the Black Struggle", 1985). As a result, the terminology and approach have become gradually more sophisticated and a common language of "race" awareness has proliferated.

In the main, three developments can be charted on the current progress of training on anti-racism.

(a) *Modified RAT*

In this there is a change in terminology to incorporate some of the "buzz" words of anti-racism, with a "softer" delivery of training (designed to reduce the "pure guilt factor" engendered by the earlier version of RAT). However, this approach retains the centrality of the individual ie the examination of racism at a personal level with "white people as the problem".

(b) *ART (Anti-Racist Training) with RAT skills*

This appears to offer serious analysis of racism based on power

39

relations. So for example, the "definition" Racism = Prejudice + Power (Judy Katz in the RAT approach) becomes slightly expanded and elaborated to include not only personal, but also institutional racism. Action is stressed and "strategies" to combat institutional racism, for instance, are promoted. The approach and skills of RAT are still retained through raising the "consciousness" of individuals whose personal attitudes and behaviour are the prime focus.

(c) *Radical Anti-Racist Programme*

This approach focuses on power relations: it locates the politics of racism in the context of the socio-economic and political life of people in society. It recognises inter-relationships with material forces which also create class and gender relations and incorporates them in its understanding of exploitation and oppression. This model does not stress training per se, but anti-racist training based on this model would certainly not focus on personal attitudes. It puts the stress on changing the structure of oppression, both at an organisational and wider level in solidarity with all groups which are the victims of this oppression.

"Race" awareness is deemed particularly attractive, plausible and relevant to social work because its traditions and values lie very much in "seeing people as individuals" and as Rooney (1987 p.41, 42) argues:

"Race Awareness Training as a formal package (RAT) has struck a sympathetic chord within parts of the social work tradition: the moral as well as the functional benefits of introspection; its provision of a ritual expiation of guilt as a painful rite of initiation to a cause; its borrowings from religion of suspended critical capacity and acts of simple faith".

And on its efficacy, he comments:

"It is packaged, cheaper than resource re-distribution and it may, it just may, lead to a communal change, a warm, welcoming opening of eyes and hearts".

The popular choice for those engaged in anti-racist work has been to either join the critics or continue with RAT or ART. Given this trend, what is the role of training in relation to individual racism expressed in agencies? Individual racism is not a "natural" phenomenon, but forged and reproduced in the context of material conditions. It is given meaning because of the structural relations which exist between the dominant and minority groups *and these conditions* (see also Diagram 5.2). Individual racism is one facet of wider aspects of racism. To this extent, anti-racist training based on the politics of racism, as an "educative" exercise is necessary for a change in service delivery, particularly since the efficacy of delivery of service is limited if clients remain powerless to determine and express their needs and the service itself remains ethnocentric. So anti-racist training has a role in the day-to-day running of the service since it may ensure effective communication and assessment of needs. Anti-racist training may help to modify service delivery, but by itself cannot *create* the changes required of the service itself. Social Services staff engaged[1] should have a broad-based training in all areas relevant to the care of elders. This should include a sound analysis of racism and its impact on black elders. (CCETSW's three year proposal for social work training [QDSW] with areas of special emphasis would have made such changes possible. Despite the government's rejection of this proposal, improvements in social work education and training, of which education on the politics of racism would be a part, should not be seen as "lost" or impossible to achieve. This is also applicable to the new developments in the Certificate in Social Care (CSC) qualification for social care staff.) Further, all staff working with elders require appropriate training and it would be worth examining what proportion of each SSD's share of the £10 million, which they received from the government towards training for care of elders (for 1988/89), went into anti-racist training.[2]

The major problem with any type of anti-racist training is that it has been viewed and accepted as the panacea for eradicating racism from the system. Although anti-racist education and training (based on the politics of racism) is relevant and essential in service provision and delivery, it is often a political tool. It remains an attractive choice for authorities because of low cost (particularly as many training officers on anti-racism are section 11 appointments) and marginal effect on resource distribution.

Internal colonialism

We now briefly look at the next stage in Diagram 5.1: internal "colonialism" and its role within the functioning of racism. We commonly speak of colonialism as an *international* exploitative system based on the pursuit of profits and expansion of markets, extracting value from commodities (raw materials to finished goods) from the periphery to the metropolis. This creates and sustains economic and political control of the periphery by the colonial power. Contemporary colonialism (termed "neo") does not operate in the classical sense of a direct political domination of one country by

---

1. Thirty per cent of students on CSS courses, 10 per cent of CQSW and approximately 50 per cent on ICSC courses worked with older people in 1986 (Biggs & Hewerdine, 1988).
2. The distribution of £10 million between local authorities was determined by the number of older people in care rather than the total population of elders. Black elders do not feature in this calculation since the distribution equation begins from the status quo position!

another but in terms of conglomerates — multinationals, who predominantly originate from the metropolitan powers (Western countries and Japan, though there are some recent marginal changes in terms of the "newly industrialising countries" such as Taiwan, South Korea). Carmichael and Hamilton (1967) first suggested broad similarities between institutional racism and colonialism, but operating *internally* in the USA and resulting in the exploitation of black Americans in the economic, political and social spheres. This concept need not refer only to white-black relations, but can include the exploitation of women and other groups (just as "classical" colonialism included the exploitation of "white" Ireland, Norway and Poland).

We examined earlier how the economy's need for labour was largely satisfied by black migrant labour from British colonies. We considered the exploitation of this group and the resultant economic and social deprivation in employment, income and housing. This cycle of poverty and racism continues today (see the PSI Report 1983, CRE: Employment of Graduates 1987, Runnymede Trust 1988) with the homilies of the Thatcherite era gaining ever more credence: eg "if only they showed more willingness to integrate" (a euphemism for assimilation) or they "sponge off the state" or they are simply "lazy". In other words, the economic and social conditions of black people (and for that matter the white unemployed, the working class) can be explained away by "blaming the victim". The focus of such arguments then shifts from individual pathology to family deficiency to cultural defects ([Honeyford, Flew et al] see Gordon & Klug 1986). For example, consider the images projected of black people in Britain. The television coverage of an item on black people in West Yorkshire will often involve a mosque appearing on the screen — symbolising Bradford. This type of image creates and reinforces the "popular" association between a mosque and "too many Asians in Bradford", but does not have to be explicitly stated because of the silent association resulting from a particular stereotype.

Such television images and their equivalents in other media and institutional processes are insidious: racist views are reproduced and the exploitation of black people is ideologically justified.[1] British institutions which reproduce such attitudes (via school curricula, police training or the Queen's "leadership" of the *Old* and *New* Commonwealth) are not necessarily organisations. This point needs to be underlined because much

---

1. For further insights see Gordon and Rosenberg *Daily Racism: The Press and Black People in Britain* (Runnymede Trust, 1989); the media coverage of the Rushdie affair gives further credence to the points above.

literature on racism equates "institutions" and organisations. "Non-organisational" social institutions are nevertheless powerful in forming views on matters such as "the impending threat to the British way of life resulting from the immigration of non-British persons". There is a dim foreboding associated with "curry and chips", but a sense of acceptability as the "British cuppa" gives way to American coke. (Perhaps if there were a few more Indian multinationals . . .) It is to the continuous structural relationship between the dominant and oppressed groups, based on "racial" subordination in this case, that the concept of internal colonialism is applicable.

The family too as a fundamental social institution is necessary to the transmitting and functioning of "internal colonialism". It is expressed in many forms including the frequently covered "heartbreaking stories of black family oppression of women etc" (Parmar 1982), which appear in the media; it is lived (and believed) by the mass consumers; and is (perhaps) communicated by social services staff in their interaction with black clients, including black elders. The family as a social institution feeds directly into the operation of internal colonialism in its economic, political and social spheres. But as the Diagram 5.1 shows, social institutions are only one facet of institutional racism. We next consider this more fully.

Institutional racism

Carmichael and Hamilton (1967) offer an explanation of the consequences of institutional racism as:

> ". . . Birmingham, Alabama — five hundred black babies die each year because of the lack of proper food, shelter and medical facilities, and thousands more are destroyed and maimed physically, emotionally and intellectually because of conditions of poverty and discrimination in the black community, that is a function of institutional racism. . . . Institutional racism relies on the active and pervasive operation of anti-black attitudes and practices. A sense of superior group position prevails: whites are 'better' than blacks; therefore, blacks should be subordinated to whites. This is a racist attitude and it permeates the society, on both the individual and institutional level, covertly and overtly". (1967, p.20).

This led Jones (1972, cited in Williams, J, 1985) to define institutional racism as "those established laws, customs and practices which systematically reflect and produce racial inequalities in American society. If racist consequences accrue to institutional laws, customs or practices the institution is racist whether or not the individuals maintaining those practices have racist intentions". So those "established laws, customs,

43

practices" which Jones refers to, cannot be reduced and explained purely as individual or group actions. They are firmly rooted in relations of production based on exploitation and racial subordination, reproducing inequalities (Diagram 5.1 and 5.2). Williams (1985) offers us an important model of institutional racism to explain various institutional processes which generate "racial" inequality through the inter-play of "racial" class, cultural, political and professional ideologies. In the literature on institutional racism, the institution is usually taken-for-granted as having a consensual and self-explanatory view and/or is equated with organisations. We have seen from the discussion above that this is not the case given the importance of "non-organisational" social institutions, which need to be identified separately, but understood as being a key element of institutional racism. Institutional racism encompasses the social institutions as well as organisations per se, with direct and indirect inter-relationships with other "forms" of racism some of which have already been discussed. (Diagram 5.1.)

Organisational racism

Earlier we quoted some common responses which SSDs give in relation to the demands for an appropriate and adequate expansion of services by black elders. We now categorise and analyse these by using the framework of organisational racism, which can be seen as a subset of institutional racism. SSDs' responses can be subdivided into three types:

(a) Monoculturalism and the rigid application of rules.

(b) Cultural accommodation/cultural pluralism.

(c) Direct racism.

Monoculturalism and the rigid application of rules as racism

The approach of "we treat them all the same" has a certain notion of fairness, a sense of equality that is widely acceptable; but it evinces little recognition of structural inequalities. In this approach "everyone is born equal — everyone starts from the same base" — thus to differentiate in the nature of service provision is to favour, and to favour is to discriminate. This regards existing provision as satisfactory and normal, accessible to *all*. It is packaged and differences are accommodated using the dominant "base". For example, dietary provisions for diabetics are acceptable but no provisions are deemed necessary for sufferers of sickle-cell anaemia! The response of one SSD to an application for Urban Aid Funding (cited on p.34) enshrines the very essence of "normal practice" — practice which is not specifically designed to militate against black clients, but which through

44

custom and tradition not only neglects the presence of black people, but ignores the multi-dimensional nature of oppression and exploitation (see Diagram 5.2). The dominant mode of service operates on the concept of dependency, accentuating the notion of passivity because of ageing, to the detriment of self-determination by the elders. Black elders have been "inserted" into a concept of care which views all elders as a homogeneous and dependent group entitled to receive social services on the basis of established practices.

But to receive these prescribed services in the first instance is a formidable task: in the process of Referral, Assessment and Service provision Rooney (1987, p.31) says:

> "The Black elder who presents or is referred for service can go through a complicated route. There is a low likelihood of referral in the first place. Referral from family, or neighbours is dependent on them knowing that the services exist, being familiar with them and having a positive perception of them. Beyond that stage there is a complex series of filters: a primary assessment to establish that it is appropriate for the SSD to get involved, and if it is, a channelling towards either a range of home based services which help to maintain the elderly person in their home in the community (such things as home help, mobile meals, day care . . .). . . . Beyond the stage of assessment there is the range of staff who provide each service and who determine the quality of care that will be given, and there are other people who use those services, in for example an elderly person's home or day centre".

This shows that although institutional structures may not be deliberately designed to discriminate, the very nature of the structure (including "professionalism" of staff) establishes practices catering for the white majority (viewed as a uniform group) and precluding black clients. As Jones' (1972) definition of institutional racism indicated, institutional structures provide for "racial" inequality, irrespective of the organisation's intentions.

Many organisational work patterns regarding policy formulation and regulatory functions are not particularly conducive to innovative changes, let alone challenging oppressive forces to create appropriate services for all clients. The bureaucratic practices of setting up meetings, working parties, sub-working groups, feasibility studies, policy documents, committees and sub-committees and community liaison networks are all regarded as a necessary chain for consultative and decision-making processes. This process may be regarded as "efficient" for an organisation committed to radical changes but in the absence of such commitment, they act as buffers to change and at best represent a good public relations exercise, yielding no change in the service provision nor in the condition of clients. There is also the common problem of "inertia", based on notions of "if it works, it must be okay" or "there are dangers inherent in change; perhaps it is best to consider the matter further". So changes in practices, improvements or otherwise, come to be regarded as antithetical to established services, unless (in the present climate) they are enforced as a cost-cutting exercise in which case, changes are often for the worse: closures of homes and day centres. Also the operation of "professionalism" by a range of personnel, mitigates against organisational change. For example, the emphasis of individual casework as a basis for social work is unlikely to change if SSDs leave matters to the "professional staff". The institutional belief that the efficient functioning of a service is through a strict adherence to rules and regulations which take precedence over the rights and needs of clients is also likely to ensure "inertial racism". This application of rules and regulations, including the enforcement of "professionalism" can result in racist practices in the context of social services provision.

The organisation's responses to black clients' demands can reinforce other forms of racism, as suggested by Diagram 5.1. Hence, tailoring services to meet black clients requirements is synonymous with "special treatment" and this is discriminatory! A curious contradictory justification of the absence of social services for black elders results from this 'colour-blind' approach: either black elders do not exist, "workers were told that there were no files on elderly West Indians, that none were ever seen at the councils' own day centres and that therefore they didn't exist" (response given to a community association by Lambeth Council 1973, in Svedin and Gorosch-Tomlinson (1984)): or the fact that "they" don't take up these services obviously means that they do not *need* them! The latter is a self-fulfilling prophecy based on a resistance to change with an assimilationist ethos at its centre. No adjustments, changes in the system of service provision are deemed to be necessary — because over time, black people will learn the "British way of life". It is *their* language, customs and religion that are seen as the major obstacles to successful assimilation. This was the characteristic response in the '50s and '60s and so it remains today.

The argument for the rights of black clients to appropriate services is a non-starter for those who hold such views because "they" must become like "us" — and consequently the problem of racism disappears. We will briefly return to this theme under cultural accommodation. Whatever the political shade of a social service organisation the assimilation ethos, emergent in the '50s, still pervades the thinking of social service provision to black elders. Where there is progress for black elders, it predominantly lies in the voluntary sector (Norman 1985).

46

Cultural accommodation/cultural pluralism

Pressures from black groups, committed individual workers and organised local groups (see Ben-Tovim et al 1987) have forced local authorities to recognise the black presence in Britain. The response to their service needs stem essentially from the Scarmanite analysis of the '81 riots under the umbrella of "ethnic issues". Some SSDs acknowledge the existence of different cultures and the importance of understanding them in order to provide for different services. The central tenet is that black groups maintain their cultural distinctiveness and that their interests are to be satisfied in the context of cultural factors only. Black elders demands of, for example, appropriate diets, "special" recreational facilities, or any other "cultural" requirements are seen as legitimate. The response then is to provide for such culturally-sensitive services through cultural adaptations within the service itself or to provide resources to self-help groups, particularly in the area of mobile meals and day centre activities (Norman, 1985).[1]

The notions of "ethnic-sensitive" practice, with "ethnically-sensitive" staff abound in social work literature — (Cheetham, Khan, Ballard, Coombe). The problem is often understood in terms of cultural and linguistic differences; the remedy is to provide an educative exercise in cultural diversity. This process of cultural adaptation and understanding requires changes in the employment (not on the basis of fair employment practices) of specialised "race" personnel, involving black people. The employment of Section 11 workers features prominently in the organisation on the basis that "ethnic specialisation" is essential to providing an "ethnically-sensitive" service. In practice, the reality is far removed from this particular aim. If the dominant mode of service is monocultural, the employment of black staff will have limited effect in the *delivery* of the service (eg the case of Mr A, quoted earlier) while the *nature* of the service remains unchanged. Apart from employing black workers many organisations commit resources to other services, including the translation of leaflets, as "taking action on black elders": for example, in one SSD, in order to increase awareness and take-up of holidays for the elders, the organisation produced leaflets in the relevant languages. Black elders responded, but the "success" was short-lived. The service itself (the hotel in this case) was geared to serving white clients!

---

1. This echoes the notion of integration which Roy Jenkins defined as "not a flattening process of assimilation but as equal opportunities accompanied by cultural diversity, in an atmosphere of mutual tolerance" (1966).

It could be argued that the organisation would have been successful had it provided a "culturally-sound" service. But is this sufficient? In practice, "progress" has only been made where cultural accommodation is accompanied by a change in material circumstances of individual black elders. Chauhan (1988) quotes a "success" story of a black elder who became "relatively independent" once housed in a newly established Part III accommodation and used the day centre facilities, also used by the local Asian community. For this elder the new accommodation and day centre facilities were material improvements offering greater independence.

Cultural accommodation to black clients' needs has been justified both by liberalism: "the British sense of tolerance and fair play" and by the New Right who recognise "racial" and "cultural" differences as "natural":

> "I believe that a preference for one's own race is as natural as a preference for one's own family". (I. Stanbrook, quoted in Barker [1981]).

Therefore, it is deemed only "natural" to be in the company of your "own kind", sharing "common cultural values and understanding". Cultural and "racial" factors are seen as innate; racism is either seen as acceptable and not immoral because of "genuine fears" of being "swamped" with "alien" cultures or it is denied on the grounds that cultural differences create cultural hostility from the white society. Both positions relegate black people to the margins of British society with peripheral changes accommodated. It is in this context that we must frame our discussions of separate provision based on self-help in the next chapter.

Direct racism

The legal definition of direct racism, according to the Race Relations Act 1976 is:

> "Where a person treats another person less favourably on *racial grounds* than he treats, or would treat, someone else". (Section 1 (i) [original emphasis].)

Organisational practices of employment and service delivery to black elders frequently display cases of direct racism and in some authorities it provides the basis for policies to counter "racial harassment". We considered earlier the complex organisational task of procedures faced by black elders before they receive a service from the SSD (p.75). Many personnel are involved in this process who have considerable discretion, particularly those in positions of power and authority (eg managers) to determine the final result.[1]

The values mentioned in our discussion of individual and organisational racism, particularly in the context of monoculturalism, underlie the ideas

48

and practices of direct racism: a denial of the black presence or, alternatively, a recognition of the black presence, but denial of different services. The transmission of various mythologies associated with, for example, the black family, permits organisations to justify the treatment of black elders as non-persons, incapable of learning "our way of life" — culturally and mentally defective — and thus racially inferior.

Concluding remarks

The different aspects of organisational racism are not discrete forms but inextricably linked. For instance, direct racism is often couched in the theory of assimilation or even integration as many of our examples showed. Institutional racism provides us with an understanding of the complexity of bureaucratic/procedural, professional, socio-economic, political and historical factors which explain how care for elders is determined and organised within the social services. However, institutional racism, as a term, is popular in social work because it offers a refuge for many seeking immunity from the attacks of personalised racism (Rooney 1987). It has also been adopted by both the Left and Right. It is used as a political slogan to describe organisations' work methods and procedures in order to explain "racial" inequalities, so keeping the level of analysis at a particular level, thereby ignoring fundamental factors — the structural relations which maintain institutional racism:

> "... the way the different structures *work together* so as to reproduce the class relations of the whole society in a specific form on an extended scale; and we have been noting the way race, as a structural feature of each sector in this complex process of social reproduction, serves to 'reproduce' that working class in a racially stratified and internally antagonistic form". (Hall et al 1978, p.346).

The diagram below, 5.2, summarises the perspective taken in this chapter in locating the response of SSDs to the needs of black elders.

---

1. For example, Chauhan (1988) cites the case of an elderly Gujerati woman who was advocated home help services by a Principal Case Worker on sound professional advice. She did not receive this service because of the *attitude* of the key gatekeeper within an organisation. The important point here is that even where the rules may work in the favour of the black client, individual racism by a person with power can thwart the correct action.

Diagram 5.2: *The position of black elders in the structure of British society*

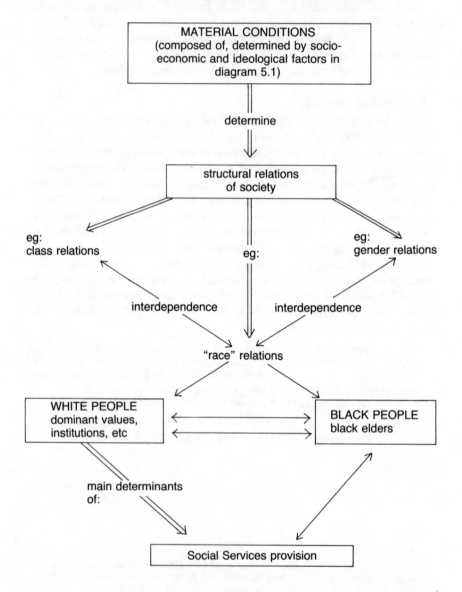

6. A separate or mainstream existence?

This chapter first considers briefly the type of services provided by the growing black voluntary projects which have emerged in response to the failure of SSDs to provide satisfactory services to black elders. It then considers whether such initiatives as a separate system of care should be adopted as the best approach to satisfying black elders' needs. Finally, our analysis of care provision and racism, will provide a set of principles, essential in planning and organising services which emancipate black elders.

Black voluntary sector

While the informal care sector (relatives, friends, neighbours) continues to play a major role in supporting black elders' needs (Leicester, Coventry, Birmingham Surveys), a growing number of self-help projects in the voluntary sector have been set up by community organisations, individual black workers within social and community work and black elders themselves. It is necessary to qualify the voluntary sector as 'black" because historically this has been the development of self-help initiatives, outside of the SSDs and the established voluntary sector which have provided care for the white communities. Like the SSDs, traditional voluntary agencies are also characterised by a low take-up of their services because of their neglect of black elders' requirements. However, a few established voluntary agencies (eg Pensioners' Link) have begun to respond to black clients in recent years.

To date, there exists no national survey on the scale and scope of the black voluntary sector concerned with elders. Norman's (1985) research provides us with the most extensive information. Black voluntary projects range from luncheon and social clubs, day centres to sheltered housing developments. With regard to domiciliary care, elders are provided with lunches either prepared by themselves on the premises or supplied by appropriate restaurants or specialist bulk suppliers. Many such clubs provide not only meals, but a convenient place for informal meetings, as well as some social activities. Some projects also plan for taking meals to those housebound; or transport is provided to bring them to the centre where they can interact with other elders rather than eat alone (Nottingham). We examined, earlier, the lack of information and knowledge of welfare rights and services. We also acknowledged the need for black elders to have advice and counselling services (for problems of isolation; "racial" harassment; generational problems within the family etc). Norman's study (1985) found that in the absence of agencies specialising in advice and counselling, various religious/cultural organisations as well as individuals undertook this task. Those involved had little training and "expertise" to provide a complete service (which is complex and ever-changing). The established voluntary agencies could address this information gap quite successfully. With their existing established system of advisory work (eg on improving service take-up and welfare rights) they are better placed to *extend* their service to black people. Some black voluntary agencies already involve Citizens Advice Bureaux (CABs) etc to provide such information.

Ageism denies elders, black and white, access to education and an intellectually stimulating life. Adult education can play a large part for this section of the community.[1] There are a few examples of multi-cultural literature provided by the Library Services with an emphasis on outreach work (Tooting Library is such an example and is cited in Norman, 1985, p.113).

Day Centres also provide a range of activities from crafts, language classes, religious practices, dominoes, cards, watching videos to providing information and advice. There are also examples of an "inter-generational-mix" with young people encouraged to use and participate in the centres' activities. There is a range in the nature of facilities provided, from suitable permanent premises to poor temporary locations; some centres are open five days a week, others only half or one day a week.

Although many regard the idea of residential care of "old people's home" as abhorrent, in Chapter 3 we showed the need for sheltered and residential housing by black elders. Two important projects are worth citing here:

---

1. A self-help group called University of the Third Age (U3A) described as "Open University for the over 50s without the exams", has its largest branch in Huddersfield, catering for 2,000 older people (Whitwam 1988). As a recent innovation (established four years ago) it would be necessary to ask how far "learning for pleasure" educational activities within U3A, involve black older people as tutors and students; as well as serving a cross-section of older people across class and gender divides.

Asian Sheltered Residential Association (ASRA GLHA Ltd) is a registered housing association initially set up as a voluntary organisation. It provides for "50 units of sheltered accommodation in Greater London, while a sister organisation (ASRA Housing Association Ltd) has developed a number of similar schemes in the Midlands" (Smith, 1988). These units are based within the Asian community, with residents living in separate units to meet individual requirements. Another housing project is Liverpool's Grouped Housing Scheme, ie "group living with support" which is regarded as an alternative to Part III accommodation and was initially offered to Somali elders (nominated by the Somali Association). The success factor here was that once the housing stock was available, the flexibility of the project allowed for the involvement of the Somali community at the planning, design and organisation stages. The Scheme's expansion has now allowed other black communities to be housed in such group-living-with-support based projects (see Benson, 1986).

This brief resumé of community-based separate voluntary projects shows how, in the absence of SSD services, black elders' obvious needs are being met. This does not imply that their needs are being met adequately. We can draw some common strands from the available literature.

Most projects are small-scale, often at the initial "experimental" phase and therefore cannot be expected to serve *all* black elders in the country. Nor can they reach *all* sections of the black elders, eg frail elderly and the disabled. Blakemore explains how Asian voluntary agencies, in order to:

"respond to a *visible* demand for social facilities from old men — has rather narrowly defined the goals and activities provided. While responding to consumer demand has certainly met some needs, if only to provide meeting places, it has also meant that other groups of old Asians (in particular women and housebound) have been left in the background". (Ibid 1985, p.178, my emphasis).

Moreover, neither can these projects be expected to provide a complete comprehensive range of services as required by the elders.

Most projects are in premises which belong to a "parent" minority organisation (in church halls, community centres or buildings owned by the "parent" organisation). This therefore determines the growth and development of services for older people (many facilities were initially designed and catered for younger people). Norman (1985); Blakemore (1985).

Since the self-help projects developed in response to the neglect of black elders' care by the primary providers, such projects have generally established separate and specialised services for different black groups.

These groups are broad-based "ethnic" groups (ie Afro-Caribbean/Asian/Chinese/Cypriots etc); rather than narrowly defined by for example, "island-differences" or "religious differences"; though "specialist" projects for specific black groups should not be discounted.

As the labour market permanently keeps those over 50 years of age out of the current employment crisis, and long-term unemployment for black people features prominently, the projects do not have a bar on those under "pensionable age". As a result of the mix of the age-groups, the demand for services is thereby increased.

Most self-help projects rely on temporary sources of funding including inner city and urban programme funds, Section 11 and Training Commission (formerly the MSC) for staff salaries. Not only are the funds temporary (and short-term), there are usually several funding agencies involved, including partnerships with local authorities and voluntary organisations as well as personal contributions of community members. Thus the problem of staff shortages are exacerbated by the lack of future funds on a regular basis.[1] Attracting funds is not only a resource-consuming activity, but may falter in the absence of "know-how" of the complex funding system. The uncertainty of funding can also generate staffing problems which the projects, already over-stretched, can ill-afford. Hence many projects are struggling to survive rather than expanding to meet the growing demands of black elders (Norman 1985).

Despite these problems, many individual case studies of projects show considerable "success" (given the immense contribution of individual workers and elders) in meeting some obvious needs of black elders. As Lalljie comments:

> "Black self-help organisations have, with minimal funding if at all, provided facilities which black elders feel to be fitting, where they can feel comfortable and where facilities have been geared to their needs. It is the existence of such facilities that have rendered black elders visible: without them, these elders would have remained scattered and invisible". (Quoted in Glendenning & Pearson 1988, p.55).

Should the care of black elders be provided by separate services?

Given the progress made by self-help projects, it would be tempting to say that if the questions of funding, staffing, and inadequate premises were

---

1. Blakemore (1985) explains that there are variations in sources of finance between Afro-Caribbean and Asian projects: differences with regard to the number of voluntary agencies involved and the role of the SSD (particularly in the meals provision).

solved, black elders' needs would be best provided by black voluntary projects. Some SSDs have forged relationships with black voluntary agencies, particularly in the context of "special meals": in order to satisfy demand by black elders, the SSD provides funds for a black voluntary agency to cater for such a demand.[1] The agency is satisfied as it has secured the necessary funds to supply such a service; the SSD has satisfied its responsibility in providing this service to black clients. The black elders' needs of meals have been met. On the surface, all three groups have managed "satisfaction" with this arrangement. However, beneath surface appearances, the mainstream service has remained untouched and indifferent to black clients, continuing its ethnocentric focus of service provision. We need to ask how effective this provision has been in terms of the alternatives available, and to question whether the SSDs should provide a comprehensive or a limited range of services, discharged via self-help projects.

In practice, Blakemore argues that the SSDs, in the majority of cases, have played a "background role in the development of projects for the minority old . . . services 'in kind' (eg transport, special meals, professional advice) rather than as funds granted on a permanent basis . . ." (1985, p.186). So a complete financial package for self-help schemes would be thwarted in the current financial crisis (rate-capping by central government); and service provision is likely to remain partial rather than comprehensive since investment in housing, for example, requires greater resource input.

Nonetheless, because of the visible gap which is partially filled by the black voluntary projects, the efforts and debates are often geared to ensuring the expansion of this sector by various community groups and often supported by the SSDs. The long history of neglect and unmet needs makes the short-term "solution" presented by self-help projects an attractive proposition, especially because of their approach in creating a social environment which allows elders' needs to be met in a relatively dignified way. However, the strong temptation to promote black voluntary projects as the providers of care for the black elders *must* be resisted in order to create a service which allows for elders to exercise their civil rights in the most humane and dignified way. This can only be achieved if the service challenges exploitative and oppressive relations which engender dependency and a worthless old age.

---

1. It cannot be assumed either that *all* self-help projects, servicing black elders, will be able to enter into such arrangements. Access to such a provision is dependent upon the representations different black groups make to the SSDs.

Principles

Determined by the framework and analysis of racism which we developed earlier the following points form the basis for principles of service provision to black elders.

● The voluntary sector has traditionally played an important role in the welfare service system, complementing the primary providers of care, the SSDs — hence in effect these voluntary agencies have adopted a *secondary* role. The black voluntary agencies catering for black elders are playing a *substitute* role and hence have become the *primary* providers of care. This role change is crucial if we argue for increasing support for them on a long-term basis, which takes us to the next point of marginalisation.

● The existence of self-help projects as a short-term solution to growing unmet needs, if supported further, not only removes the pressure on SSDs to develop appropriate services for a multi-racial society, but it becomes incorporated in the "system" as the *best* approach. A short-term solution, even if it is partial, becomes a long-term pattern established to provide second rate domiciliary care, day centres and possibly housing. In other words, a "fringe provision" is permanently created with temporary structures which in a climate of financial stringencies is the first to be cut, rather than the mainstream services.

● SSDs cannot argue that self-help projects have emerged and are encouraged because of existing financial constraints. What happened in the '60s and '70s to the service provision for black clients? Neither period witnessed any significant tightening of the public purse as at present. The cost-minimisation rationale prevalent in *today's* SSDs has resulted in serious deficiencies in care, particularly for black elders because of the marginal services they receive[1] creating *de facto* discrimination against black groups as opposed to white clients. It is not only a matter of a cheap service but also of the marginalisation of black people. Since SSDs, like other state institutions, regard black elders as having a marginal existence within this society, the margins can be trimmed, cut or maintained (through the support of marginal institutions such as self-help projects). Separate projects are supported and positively viewed by the SSDs because they provide a "buffer" against direct criticism of SSDs' failure to provide services. They act as the "interface" between the SSDs and a potential black political struggle by elders to exercise their civil rights (John, 1981).

---

1. This situation particularly arises because of SSDs' past neglect of care to black elders results in developing approprite services from a very low base (or a zero-base).

56

● Some observers (Hopkins, 1987) misguidedly suggest that separate services are an alternative to statutory provision. An alternative implies a choice in the matter and free entry to the latter statutory sector. But various forces (eg racism in its many forms, linguistic difficulties, bureaucratic blockages/referrals) act as barriers against the potential use of statutory provision by black clients. The choice cannot be effectively exercised within existing services. Indeed it is precisely this lack of entry which initiated black self-help groups (as a *response* to the *failure* of SSDs to change).

● A separate and specialist service for black elders is essentially determined by notions of culture and identity. We are presented with separate day centres for the Afro-Caribbean; "Asian"; Chinese; Cypriots; and so on — all "ethnically" determined to secure and promote "ethnic" identity (Sivanandan, 1983). Cultural beliefs and practices are important and in particular act as a source of strength in a hostile society. However, to reduce "race" and racism to cultural absolutism denies the structural context (Diagram 5.1 and 5.2 in Chapter 5), and shares directly the New Right's view of "kith and kin" — "it is only natural to be with your own cultural groups" (as though pluralistic separation can be hermetically sealed).

● Apart from the New Right's cultural nationalism, its ideology of voluntarism and "privatisation" of care converge with the notions of separate and specialist service for black elders. The New Right's view is that welfare maximisation of the individual[1] is best determined by maximising individual liberty ("freedom of choice") with the guiding principles of profit maximisation in the private sector[2] — *or* by minimalist state intervention to encourage voluntarism within the family and/or in the Voluntary Sector, as the ideal principle of care for the individual (David, 1986).

Concluding remarks

We have shown that separate and specialist services provide the means to justify this view that black people have a marginal existence in British society. In consequence, marginal institutions can provide all the adequate and appropriate services to black elders, if only they were sufficiently

---

1. The New Right's emphasis on the individual is illustrated by Margaret Thatcher's recent comment that there is no such thing as society — only individuals exist.
2. The government's commitment to private care is reflected in the private sector's share of residential places in England and Wales which "had risen from 29 per cent in 1979 to 43 per cent in 1984, whereas the number of local authority residents has remained stable over the same period. It is estimated that if current trends continue, half the beds in residential and nursing homes will be in the private and voluntary sector within six years" (Biggs, 1987).

resourced. Our analysis has shown that "race" and racism are important features of structural inequalities and hence the primary objective of black people (elders included) is to confront and dismantle those structures which assign them to a marginal existence. Black elders can then determine and define what are the "adequate and appropriate" services *within* the context of state provision. It is the responsibility of SSDs to provide services for older people: **black elders are part of this society and hence entitled to mainstream services.**[1] The service designed to address black elders' needs (determined by them and located in their experience which is historically and structurally based) must ensure that the methods developed allow black elders to fight "racial" subordination.

---

1. Groups like SCEMSC, Age Concern etc, have a large part to play in campaigning for a radical change in the service provision as well as in improving incomes for the elders. The redistribution of a recent tax cut of £2 billion for the top rate taxpayers would have ensured greater financial independence for the elders. Further, one in four elders could stay in their own home, if adequate support services were available (*The Guardian* 19.5.88). How far the Griffiths' recommendations for Community Care and the Wagner Report on residential care will influence the States' concept of care remains to be seen.

Postscript

During 1988, the year when this book was researched and written, there were significant developments. Sir Roy Griffiths presented his report on community care, reaffirming local authority SSDs' central authority in community care — to the government's alarm. On training, the government rejected the proposed "Care for Tomorrow", QDSW, the three year qualifying training award for social work. The re-structuring of care for the "elderly, people with a mental handicap and people with mental illness" was also being quietly shaped by the government. In 1989 it finally announced that it would implement some of the major proposals of Griffith's report. This was followed shortly by the introduction of the community care bill "Caring for People Community Care in the next decade and beyond" in November, which received its second reading before Christmas.

All major reforms are guided by specific considerations — humanitarian, ideological or financial. To understand the basis for the timing and content of the community care bill we need to examine three central issues. First, the demographic changes cannot be ignored: the elderly population will more than double by the year 2025. Second, in 1986 the Audit Commission report, *Making a Reality of Community Care*, stated that the primary focus for many SSDs' community care policy was institutionalisation and was less concerned with meeting clients' needs effectively. Most particularly the "perverse" financial incentives of using social security payments to place people in private residential care caused an explosion in private sector provision. In 1979 the cost of this was estimated at £10 million compared to £1 billion a year in 1989 — a massive 10,000 per cent increase. As a result private sector provision of residential care exceeds that of the public sector (estimated at 231,800 beds compared to 215,400 in SSD homes and NHS hospitals with 50,400 beds provided by voluntary organisations, according to a market survey published by Laing and Buisson). Third, in line with its other policies whether in manufacturing or welfare sectors, over the last ten years the government sought large private sector activity in the *direct* supply of care for elders.

If the provisions outlined in the White Paper come into effect, the "perverse" financial incentives above will come to an end in April 1991, but the position of elders already resident in homes before April 1991 will be protected. The White Paper's function is to re-structure health services to the mentally ill, elders and the mentally handicapped by determining how they are *delivered and being funded*. The key objectives underlying this are to ensure:

1. Services directed to increase stay at home;
2. support for carers;
3. local authorities' co-ordinating role in conjunction with medical nursing and other interests, for assessment of individual need and the design and delivery of care packages with "available resources";
4. increased ("maximum use") role of the independent sector;
5. clarification of responsibility of agencies for accountability and performance purposes;
6. new funding structure for social care.

The White Paper further specifies (p.5, 1.10):

"1. Services that respond flexibly and sensitively to the needs of individuals and carers;
2. services that allow a range of options for consumers;
3. services that intervene no more than is necessary to foster independence;
4. services that concentrate on those with the greatest needs."

To carry this out, "the government is seeking to establish the right financial and managerial frameworks which will help to secure the delivery of good quality local services in line with national policy objectives" (p.4, 1.7).

The role of the local authority is then one of "arrangers and purchasers of care services rather than monopolistic providers" (p.17). In other words to become "enabling authorities", local authorities will experience a major structural shift from a *provider* to a *purchaser*, resulting in greater competition, choice, case management, and presumably cheap services — tailored to meet individual need. However, dual economy, ie the co-existence of public and private sectors in the purchaser-providing model can only meet the bill's well sounding sentiments if:

(a) As Griffiths proposed, the funding to local authorities is increased and "ring fenced" to finance community care that is constructed with the independent sector (ie the private sector) at agreed prices.

(b) the independent sector is willing to respond to "the value of contracts" in a competitive market. Thus priority may most likely be given to elders who are in a position to pay their own fees for residential care (estimated at 40 per cent). According to Laing and Buisson's review, only 28 per cent of nursing homes charge fees for shared rooms which can be met from social security payments alone — while "in some areas of the country the percentages approach zero". However as the owner of Care at Home — a private home care services agency — stated: "When people suggest that private companies should tender for public sector care work, they have to recognise that the level of funding available in the public sector is ludicrously low. The government and public must appreciate that proper quality community care is not a cheap option" (*Financial Times* 18 December 1989).

In other words the result would be a two tier service in the private sector, but more importantly, in the absence of adequate funding, a *real* decline in the services demanded by elders — with consequent increase in care at home (incidentally an objective of this bill).[1] This is because the budgetary controls set on funding directed as it is through the rate support grant, make it difficult to assess whether funding is adequate or not. Setting budgets is never a neutral activity: setting an arbitrary figure without reference to the nature or volume of met and unmet needs, implies that services to elders is a low priority. This is particularly so when one of the requirements of delegated budgets is that there must be a balanced budget at the end of the year (no overspending in total).

Community care and black elders

The analysis offered in the last six chapters may lead to the conclusion that the alarm caused by the increased private sector role is not an issue for black elders. After all what have they gained from the public domain? What is there to be gained? Is the issue about achieving a better share in the private sector (referred to as the independent sector in the bill) or a change in the mainstream services in the public sector? I concluded in the last chapter that the objective was to change the mainstream services in the public sector to provide for better care for *all* people — *all* elders.

---

1. "It is estimated that around six million people are involved in the regular provision of care — with 1.4 million of these devoting more than 20 hours a week to the task — and carers' organisations calculate that this is saving the state £15 billion a year" (*Financial Times* 18.12.89).

The central emphases of the bill rest on:

(a) the assessment of individual needs;
(b) the determination of care packages;
(c) consumer choice — self determination;
(d) competition to ensure the provision of better services.

In the context of social service provision for black elders the question of assessing individual needs and devising care packages assumes centrally that these are recognised; that black elders have "entered the market" for social care and thus the assessment, identification and provision of services can be arranged. Stereotyping, gatekeeping, organisational and direct racism effectively work to keep black elders *out* of the "market". Racism creates an effective barrier to entry to social service provision, and eliminating these barriers is essential before one begins to talk about "community care" as in the White Paper. In the analysis of market dynamics, the interplay between demand and supply assumes that black elders are willing, able and can effectively express their *demand* for care provision; while the suppliers, that is the providers (the private and voluntary sectors) can supply accessible, appropriate and adequate services to them. This is essential for the determination of care packages: assessing what is required, in what form and who can supply it — at a particular price. Given the earlier evidence of great levels of *unmet collective needs*, where will the case managers begin in their specified role of arranging community care package? (p.21, 3.3.4). Will this be at cost-benefit analysis work, purchasing, budgetting, forecasting or planning stage? Will they develop new services and redistribute resources to increase the low (or even zero) base services from where black elders start? Regarding consumer choice and self determination, again one assumes this will not only be articulated by individual black elders, but that the case managers/staff have the required skills and knowledge to translate that choice into services.

Certainly CCETSW's new Social Work Award — the Diploma in Social Work — incorporates for the first time regulations on anti-racism as requirements for this qualification. It is also anticipated that anti-racism regulations will appear on the other two levels, that is, Social Care and Post-qualifying Studies (PQS). It can be hoped that, training-wise at least, newly qualified staff will have some grounding in anti-racism and the capacity to work with black elders, but what is to be done with existing personnel? We need training arrangements (3.1.4) to address their lack of appropriate knowledge and skills.

Finally there is the issue of competition. Chapter 6 describes the position of black voluntary organisations as the main providers of appropriate services to black elders — on shoestring budgets. To engage in competition in the "marketing" for services, not only is information of the "market" required but also substantial skills to tender, contract, budget, plan and utilise resources. Hence structurally, black voluntaries are the "weak players" in any competitive tender to provide for services to black elders at a competitive price to the SSDs. It could be argued, as the experience of the last eight years shows, that the word "competition" will be uttered, but not practiced as in the case of (the privatised) British Telecom. If this is the case, at least financial and budgetary management may help to better harness public resources in the control of SSDs. However the White Paper only afforded 57 words (compared to 75 in the Griffiths report!) to "people from ethnic minorities" (2.9 p.10 and 11). It said:

> "The government recognised that people from different cultural backgrounds have particular care needs and problems. Minority communities may have different concepts of community care and it is important that service providers are sensitive to these variations. Good community care will take account of the circumstances of minority communities and will be planned in consultation with them".

As discussed earlier, being "sensitive" and "consulting minorities" is not sufficient to ensure that necessary services will be provided to black elders. This is particularly the case when we know that the "market" is a poor servant in the allocation of services according to people's needs.

Sir Griffiths went slightly further in his report and talked of "action", "policy", "responsibility of social services authority" and the need for "training". Certainly the Social Services Inspectorate in their role of approving community care plans from April 1991, have offered some encouragement in this regard. It remains to be seen how far this is implemented.

Meanwhile for black elders, the community care bill promises not only more of the same but perhaps a worse scenario of service provision in a highly restrictive, chaotic and ever shrinking welfare society — unless care managers are equipped and committed to black elders needs; and black voluntaries are resourced to move from a "weak" to a competitive position in providing services to black elders.

Bibliography

ADSS and CRE, *Multi-Racial Britain: The Social Services Responses*, A Working Party Report, 1978.

Age Concern/Help The Aged Housing Trust, *Housing for Ethnic Elders*, Age Concern, 1984.

Barclays Review, "World Population 1950-2025", Vol.LIX, No.1, February 1984.

Barker, J, *Research Perspectives on Ageing: Black and Asian old people in Britain*, (Manchester and London Survey), Age Concern Research Unit, 1984.

Barker, M, *The New Racism*, Junction Books, 1981.

Barr, H, *Perspectives on Training for Residential Work*, CCETSW Study 8, 1987.

Benson, S, "Somali Sanctum", *Community Care*, 3 July, 1986.

Ben-Tovim, G, et al, *The Local Politics of Race*, Macmillan, 1986.

Berry, S, et al, *Report on a Survey of West Indian Pensioners in Nottingham*, Nottingham SSD, 1981.

Bhalla, A, and Blakemore, K, *Elders of the Minority Ethnic Groups*, (Birmingham Survey), AFFOR, 1981.

Biggs, S, "Quality of Care and the Growth of Private Welfare for Old People", *Critical Social Policy*, 1988.

Biggs, S, and Hewerdine, C, *Older People: a resource list for Social Work trainers*, CCETSW, 1988.

Blakemore, K, "The State, the Voluntary Sector and New Developments in Provision for the Old of Minority Racial Groups", *Ageing and Society* 5, 1985.

Brennan, J, and McGeevor, P, *Employment of Graduates from Ethnic Minorities*, CRE, 1987.

Brindel, D, "MPs Criticise Care for Elderly", *The Guardian*, 19 May, 1988.

Brown, C, *Black and White: The third PSI survey*, Heinemann, 1984.

Carmichael, S, and Hamilton, C.V, *Black Power: the politics of liberation in*

America, Pelican, 1967.

Centre for Contemporary Cultural Studies, *The Empire Strikes Back: race and racism in '70s Britain*, Hutchinson University Library, 1982.

CCETSW Paper 30, *DipSW Requirements and Regulations for the Diploma in Social Work*, 1989.

Chauhan, B, "Black Elderly — Service Delivery and Service Planning" in Mossadaq, M, and Froggatt, 1988.

Cheetham, J, et al (ed.), *Social and Community Work in a Multi-Racial Society*, Harper & Row, 1981.

Coombe, V, and Little, A. (ed), *Race and Social Work: a guide to training*, Tavistock Publications, 1986.

Cooper, J, "Elderly West Indians in Leicester, 1978", in Glendenning, F. (ed) 1979 and in Cheetham, J, et al, 1981.

Cox, O.C, *Caste, Class and Race: a study in social dynamics*, MR, 1948.

CRC Report, *Urban Deprivation: racial inequality and social policy*, CRC Reference Division (London), 1976.

CRE, *Racial Equality in Social Services Departments: a survey of Equal Opportunity Policies in England, Scotland and Wales*, 1989.

David, M, "Moral and Maternal, The Family in the New Right", in Levitas, R, (ed) 1986.

Davies, A, "Elderly, British and Black", *Voluntary Action*, 13, 1982.

Denney, D, "Some Dominant Perspectives in the Literature Relating to Multi-Racial Social Work", *British Journal of Social Work*, 13:149-174, 1983.

Dowd, J.J, and Bengtson, V.L, "Ageing in Minority Populations: an examination of the Double Jeopardy Hypothesis", *Journal of Gerontology*, 33, 1978.

Duffield, M, *Black Radicalism and the Politics of De-industrialism: the hidden history of Indian foundry workers*, Gower, 1988.

Farrah, M, *Black Elders in Leicester: an action research report on the needs of black elderly people of African descent from the Caribbean*, Leicester SSD, 1986.

Fenton, S, *Ageing Minorities: Black people as they grow old in Britain*, CRE, 1987.

File, N, and Power, C, *Black Settlers in Britain 1955-1958*, Heinemann Educational Books, 1981.

Fryer, P, *Staying Power: the history of black people in Britain*, Pluto Press, 1984.

Gilroy, P, *There Ain't No Black in the Union Jack: the cultural politics of race and nation*, Hutchinson, 1987.

Gilroy, P, *Problems in Anti-Racist Strategy*, Runnymede Trust, 1987.

Glendenning, F, (ed), *The Elders in Ethnic Minorities*, Beth Johnson Foundation, 1979.

Glendenning, F, and Pearson, M, *The Black and Ethnic Minority Elders in Britain: health needs and access to services*, Working Papers on the Health of Older People No.6, Health Education Authority and Keele University, 1988.

Gordon, P, and Klug, F, *New Right New Racism*, Searchlight, 1986.

Grant, L, "Black Elderly, the Caribbean Perspective", in Mossadaq, M, and Froggatt, A, 1988.

Griffiths, R, *Community Care: Agenda for Action*, a report to the Secretary of State for Social Services, HMSO, 1988.

Hall, S, et al, *Policing the Crisis: mugging, the state, and law and order*, Macmillan, 1978.

Hall, S, "Race, articulation and societies structured in dominance" in *Sociological Theories: race and colonialism*, UNESCO, 1989.

Hall, S, "Introduction" in *Forty Winters on: memories of Britain's post war Caribbean immigrants*, Lambeth Council, 1988.

HMSO, The White Paper "Caring for People, Community Care in the next decade and beyond — caring for the 1990s", Cm 844, November 1989.

Holland, B, and Lewando-Hundt, G, *Coventry's Ethnic Minority Elderly Survey: method, data and applied action*, 1986.

Home Office, *Racial Discrimination, a guide to the Race Relations Act 1976*.

Hopkins, J, "Alternative services which aim to affirm an ethnic identity", *Social Work Today*, 23 November 1987.

Hospers, J, *An Introduction to Philosophical Analysis*, RKP, 1978.

Husband, C, "Culture, context and practice: racism in Social Work" in *Radical Social Work and Practice*, Brake, M, and Bailey, R, E, Arnold, 1980.

Husband, C, "Notes on Racism in Social Work Practice", *Multi-Racial Social Work*, 1, 1980.

Husband, C, "Racism, Prejudice, and Social Policy" in Coombe, V, and Little, A, (ed) 1986.

Institute of Race Relations, *The Fight against Racism*, Book 4, 1986.

Jagucki, W, "The Polish Experience: 40 years on" in *The Psychological Problems of Refugees*, Baker, R, (ed) 1983.

Jenkins, R, "Address given by the Home Secretary to a meeting of Voluntary Liaison Committee", 23 May, 1966.

John, G, "Social and Community Work in Specific Settings, 1", in *The Open University*, Block 7, Units 21, 22, 23, 1978.

Jolley, M, "Ethnic Minority Elders Want More Sensitive Services", *Social Work Today*, 14 January, 1988.

Klein, R, "The old blacks beat the blues", *Community Care*, 4 January, 1979.

Lees, P, and Gardiner, S, *Elderly Ethnic Minorities*, Age Concern, 1974.

Levitas, R, (ed), *The Ideology of the New Right*, Polity Press, 1986.

Lewando-Hundt, G, and Grant, L, "Studies of Black Elders — an exercise in window dressing or the groundwork for widening provision" (Coventry Survey) in *Social Services Research* No.s.5 and 6, 1987.

Lim, S.P, "The Chinese Elders in Camden; their needs and hopes" in Glendenning, F, (ed), 1979.

Lyn, I.L, *The Chinese Community in Liverpool: their unmet needs with respect to education, social welfare and housing*, Merseyside Area Profile Group, 1982.

May, N, "Elderly South Asians in Britain". A survey of relevant literature and themes for future research. *Ageing and Society*, Vol.3, pt.1, 1983.

McNabb, K, and Psacharopoulos, G, "Racial Earnings Differentials in the UK", *Oxford Economic Papers*, Vol.33, No.3, 1981.

McNeely, R.L, and Colen, J.L, "Ageing in Minority Groups", *Sage Focus Editions*, 61, 1983.

Miles, R, *Racism and Migrant Labour*, RKP, 1982.

Mossadaq, M, and Froggatt, A, *Black and Asian Elders — do our services deliver?* A report of proceedings of the Conference at Bradford University, 7 January, 1988.

Murray, N, "The central issue is racism", *Community Care*, 28 February, 1985.

NISW, *The Griffiths Task Force: race dimension*, Race Equality Unit, 1989.

Norman, A, *Triple jeopardy: growing old in a second homeland*, Centre for Policy on Ageing, Policy Studies on Ageing, No.3, 1985.

Norton, A, et al, *Councils of care: planning a local government strategy for older people*, Centre for Policy on Ageing, Policy Studies on Ageing, No.5, 1986.

Open University, "Migration and Settlement in Britain", E354, Block 1, Units 2 & 3, 1982.

Patel, H.J, "Accentuate the Positive . . ." *Community Care*, 5 June, 1986.

Parmar, P, *Gender, race and class: Asian women in resistance*, in CCCS (1982).

Pheonix, A, "The Afro-Caribbean Myth", *New Society*, 4 March, 1988.

Ramdin, R, *The Making of the Black Working Class in Britain*, Wildwood House, 1987.

Rooney, B, *Racism and Resistance to change: A study of the Black Social Workers Project — Liverpool Social Services Department*, Merseyside Area Profile Group, 1987.

Runnymede Trust and Radical Statistics Group, *Britain's Black Population*, Heinemann Educational Books, 1980.

Shaw, C, "Latest estimates of ethnic minority populations", *Population Trends*, 51, HMSO, Spring 1988.

Sivanandan, A, "Race, Class and the State" in *A Different Hunger: writings on black resistance*, Pluto Press, 1982.

Sivanandan, A, "Challenging Racism: strategies for the 1980s", *Race and Class*, 25, 2, 1-11, 1983.

Sivanandan, A, "RAT and the Degradation of the Black Struggle", *Race and Class*, 26, 4, 1-33, 1985.

Smith, D.J, *Racial Disadvantage in Britain: the PEP Report*, Penguin, 1977.

Smith, P, "Meeting the Housing Needs of Elderly Asian People", *Social Work Today*, 4 February, 1988.

Social Trends, 18, HMSO, 1988.

SSI Survey, Hughes, R, *Policy and Practice in the North West — Part One of a Two-Part Exercise*, DHSS, 1986.

SSI Survey, Prime, R, *Developing Social Services for Black and Ethnic Minority Elders in London — Overview Report and Action Plan*, DHSS, 1987.

Standing Conference of Ethnic Minority Senior Citizens, *Making a reality of Residential Care for Ethnic Minority Elderly*, SCEMSC, 1987.

Stanley, K, *The needs of the Black Elderly in Leeds*, Ethnic Elders Steering Group, Leeds Federated Housing Association, 1986.

Svedin, A.M, and Gorosch-Tomlinson, D, "They Said We Didn't Exist", *Social Work Today*, 15, 30 April, 1984.

Thompson, J, "Ageing of the population: contemporary trends and issues", *Population Trends*, 51, HMSO, Spring 1988.

Townsend, P, *The Last Refuge: a survey of residential institutions and homes for the elderly in England and Wales*, RKP, 1962.

Troyna, B, and Williams, J, *Racism, Education and the State*, Croom Helm, 1986.

Turnbull, A, *Greenwich's Afro-Caribbean and South Asian Elderly People*, Greenwich SSD, 1985.

Visram, R, *Ayahs, Lascars and Princes: Indians in Britain 1700-1947*, Pluto Press, 1986.

Wagner Report, "A Positive Choice", *Residential Care*, HMSO, 1988.

Walvin, J, *Passage to Britain*, Penguin, 1984.

Walker, A, "A State of Confusion", Provision for Old People 2; *Community Care*, 3 March, 1988.

Westwood, S, and Bachu, P, "Images and Realities", *New Society*, 6 May, 1988.

Whitwarm, L, "Boundaries falling at fifty", *Times Higher Educational Supplement*, 2 September, 1988.

Williams, J, "Redefining Institutional Racism", *Ethnic and Racial Studies*, Vol.8, No.3, 1985.

The Runnymede Trust

The Runnymede Trust is a registered educational charity set up in 1968. Its objectives are the collection and dissemination of information and the promotion of public education on immigration and race relations. This is done in a number of ways:

- An information service which provides information on race and immigration.
- A reference library of books, pamphlets and press cuttings which may be used by prior appointment.
- A monthly bulletin, *Race and Immigration*.
- Policy-oriented research projects on specific issues.
- Publication of pamphlets and papers on matters of current interest and concern.
- Seminars and meetings.

A full list of publications and details of subscriptions to *Race and Immigration* are available from the address below.

The Runnymede Trust
11 Princelet Street
London E1 6QH
Tel: 071-375 1496